THE
EXPERTSHIP GROWTH GUIDE

THE COMPREHENSIVE GUIDE TO BUILDING MEANINGFUL AND ACTIONABLE PERSONAL GROWTH PLANS FOR EXPERTS.

EXPERTUNITY
ALISTAIR GORDON & DOMINIC JOHNSON

EXPERTUNITY

AUTHORS: Alistair Gordon, Dominic Johnson
TITLE: The Expertship Growth Guide
EDITORS: Sigrid Chambers, Lynsey Chan, Graeme Philipson
ISBN NUMBER: 978-0-6481668-4-9 (eBook) 978-0-6481668-4-9 (paperback)
SUBJECTS: Management
DESIGN: Melissa Drennan, Jodie Laczko

National Library of Australia Cataloguing-in-Publication Entry

NATIONAL LIBRARY OF AUSTRALIA

A catalogue record for this
book is available from the
National Library of Australia

TABLE OF CONTENTS

WHAT CAPABILITY AM I SEEKING
TO GROW

MY ORGANIZATION

CUSTOMERS & COMPETITORS

CHANGE MANAGEMENT

STRATEGIC THINKING

INNOVATION

INTRODUCTION TO THE

EXPERTSHIP GROWTH GUIDE

We believe this is the first Guide of its kind in the world.

This book is designed by experts for experts, their leaders and growth supporters. It assists experts in becoming the very best experts they can by helping them craft meaningful and actionable Personal Growth Plans. It contains 102 growth opportunities – initiatives which, when put into action, position experts, no matter what their expert domain, to have greater impact and influence, and add more value.

GROWTH FOR EXPERTS

Many of those using this book will have participated in one of Expertunity's growth programs for experts around the world. So, you'll understand about the concept of the *Expertship Model*, and the process by which you should develop your *Personal Growth Plan* using our template.

It is however designed to be a standalone tool, so we have included chapters at the beginning of this Guide explaining these concepts. If you know about them already you can jump straight over them. If you're new to the concept you can read about how Expertship is for experts what leadership is to leaders.

THE EXPERTSHIP MODEL

The Expertship Model is a result of years of research and testing and is acknowledged as one of the leading capability frameworks for experts. Experts from places as far afield as Las Vegas, New York, London, New Delhi, Singapore, Sydney and Auckland use the model. These experts operate in a wide variety of expert domains – IT, law, HR, Engineering, Sales, Finance, Risk and Science.

THE EXPERTSHIP360

This Guide is best used in conjunction with a feedback tool, such as the *Expertship360*. Recipients of a 360 report get valuable feedback from a range of their stakeholders, and thus can determine which capabilities are their strengths to be built upon, and which capabilities present opportunities for significantly more value to be added. The growth initiatives listed in this Guide are organised by capability area.

A GUIDE FOR MANAGERS OF EXPERTS, TOO

Some readers may lead a team or division of experts. You might be responsible for helping them identify and satisfy their development needs. This Guide represents the latest thinking on how to motivate and get the best value from your experts. You may be receiving it as an accompaniment to Expertunity's *Leader of Experts* program.

TOP EXPERTS COMBINE TECHNICAL AND ENTERPRISE SKILLS

Experts face many challenges that are unique to them. Many challenges are resolved by deploying *technical skills* – skills which experts have typically been trained in many times over the years. In fact, usually nearly all of an experts' capability development has been in these technical areas.

However, the very best experts combine these technical skills with what we refer to as *enterprise skills*. These are the additional skills – such as business acumen, change agility, stakeholder management, and personal impact – which enable experts to deploy their technical skills best. Many experts have missed out on training in these skills, and the arrival of Expertship programs seeks to restore this imbalance. You can find out about all of our Expertship services at www.expertunity.global

Of course, we would love to hear your feedback on how we can continue to improve this Guide. Please let us know how you found it helpful, and how you think we could make it easier to use.

We would also love to hear your success stories putting these growth initiatives to work. Our website provides you with a direct line of contact with the authors. Good luck with your personal growth plan in 2019.

Alistair Gordon
& Dominic Johnson
March 2019

HOW TO USE THIS
GROWTH GUIDE

WHO ARE YOU?
- A participant on one of Expertunity's expertship programs?
- An expert who has completed an Expertship360 survey?
- An expert looking to develop their enterprise skills?
- A manager of a participant doing any of the above?

We have designed this Guide to be useful for all of you, but we have some specific suggestions on how to use the Guide for readers in each category below. The Guide is designed to be a reference tool, for you to dip in and out of, focusing on the growth initiatives we describe in the areas that most interest you. The Guide is not designed to read from first page to last, although this is an approach some readers take.

FINDING WHAT YOU ARE LOOKING FOR
In order to help you navigate this Guide most effectively, we have provided:
- A table of contents (like any other guide);
- An index describing the type of skills you most hope to develop; and
- A Glossary at the back of the Guide.

We hope that these three navigation tools will help you find the growth initiatives you are looking for.

ADVICE FOR EXPERTSHIP PROGRAM PARTICIPANTS

As a participant on one of Expertunity's Expertship programs, you will either be:

- Preparing to start a program; or
- Preparing to write your Personal Growth Plan (PGP), after attending an expertship workshop; or
- Revisiting your PGP as a consequence of feedback from your manager or your coach.

To further build upon your face-to face experience in our programs, you are required to complete a Personal Growth Plan which provides focus to embed new skills and knowledge learned on the program back into the way you work in the workplace. Detailed advice about writing such a plan is in the next section. This Guide provides 100 personal growth initiatives – activities and ideas by which you can master and deploy new behaviors to include in your plan. This book seeks to answer the question: "What do I do to acquire these skills and knowledge?"

Steps for action:

- Refer back to your Expertship360 report when writing, actioning and reviewing your Personal Growth Plan, as it provides a roadmap for strengths you wish to build upon, and gaps in your capability you want to address;
- Refer back to the notes you took during the workshop on opportunities for improvement, and take another look at your presentation video;
- Make a list of impact areas (for example, "Stakeholder Engagement" or "Communicating with Impact"), and use the indexes to identify the sections of this book that deal with growth initiatives in those areas;
- Select the growth initiatives that you think are most relevant to your needs, and appeal to you most. Very often you might think of something you can do that is not on our list, but in having read our suggestions, other possibilities occur to you. As long as you can measure outcomes, we encourage you to innovate; and then
- Check in with your coach briefly to share your plans and get their feedback. The Expertship coaches are expert in helping experts shape Personal Growth Plans.

ADVICE FOR EXPERTSHIP360 PARTICIPANTS

As a participant who is completing an Expertship 360 survey, you will already be working with an Expertunity Coach, and your manager to support you in interpreting your results and in creating a Personal Growth Plan. This Guide will support you in understanding the core enterprise capabilities required to reach Expert Mastery in your role and provide some targeted steps to focus specifically on your core strengths and growth areas apparent in your 360 report.

Steps for action:

- Refer back to your 360 report when actioning and reviewing your Personal Growth Plan as it provides an excellent benchmark for you to be able to measure your growth from;
- Make a list of impact areas (for example, "Stakeholder Engagement" or "Communicating with Impact"), and use the indexes to identify the sections of this book that deal with growth initiatives in those areas;
- Select the growth initiatives that you think are most relevant to your needs, and appeal to you most. Very often you might think of something you can do that is not on our list, but having read our suggestions, other possibilities occur to you. As long as you can measure outcomes, we encourage you to innovate; and then
- Check in with your coach briefly to share your plans and get their feedback. The Expertship coaches are experts in helping experts shape Personal Growth Plans.

ADVICE FOR INDIVIDUAL EXPERTS NOT ON OUR PROGRAMS

As an individual Expert looking to develop your enterprise skills, you will likely be a subject matter expert and have been provided this Guide by your manager, or HR in your organization, or you have found it by individual research (congratulations, great work!). Since you are working independently, here are some suggested actions you might want to consider in order to get the best value from both this Guide and the process.

Actions to take:

- To help inform you where to start, you may like to review and consider any data you have collected relating to your performance or your personal preferences around ways of working, including your strengths and growth opportunities. You could consider any previous performance reviews and specific growth areas that have been suggested to you, feedback from your direct Manager, your Manager's Manager, or stakeholders. If you have ever completed a profiling tool about preferred ways of working, these can often be a good place to start as well.
- Without formal feedback (via the Expertship360), ask for informal feedback from your colleagues. Include your manager and your managers' manager, your technical cohort (close working technical colleagues), and also your stakeholders – those that you do work for. What do they believe you do well, and what do they believe provides an opportunity for you to do better? Ask them to be candid, otherwise you'll get compliments and no real actionable data. It takes courage, but it is worth it.
- Do an analysis of what you think your strengths and growth opportunities are and compare this with feedback you get from others.
- Armed with these two data points, you have the opportunity to decide on two or three things to work on – we suggest completing a Personal Growth Plan which is described later in this book.
- Then follow the steps of the others listed above, choose topic areas, explore the suggestions and ideas for growth initiatives under those headings, and choose three or four actions you intend to take.
- We strongly recommend, if the relationship is positive, to validate these with your manager.

ADVICE FOR MANAGERS OF EXPERTS

As a manager of a participant on one of our expertship programs, you are supporting your direct report in becoming the best expert they can be (master expert) in their area of expertise. This Guide will help you to become familiar with the Expertship capability framework which includes both the technical and enterprise skills required to reach master expert status. In understanding the enterprise capabilities in more detail, you will be able to better support your direct report with relevant coaching, provide them with the right growth opportunities, help them measure their success and keep them focused on their goals.

Actions to take:

- Read the chapter on the Expertship model, and mentally assess your reports on where they sit under each impact area on the Expertship scale – are they operating at specialist, expert, or master expert level?
- Once you've assessed where they sit, we encourage you to have a discussion with them about where they think they sit under each level.
- You are both then ready to select a strength to build on, and several growth opportunities to address. We encourage you and your report to look at the growth initiatives listed under each capability and consider what is relevant and doable for your report.
- We would strongly recommend you require your report to complete a Personal Growth Plan and focus on how both your report and you are going to measure success. A template for such a plan is included in Appendix i, and a detailed explanation of how to complete one is in the next section.

OTHER SUGGESTIONS FOR HELPING YOU GET STARTED

The list of capabilities and roles in this Guide, when you look at them one after another, can be daunting. However, that's because the role of experts – and the number of capabilities they must master – is also daunting. As such, our capability framework has to be comprehensive, and indeed challenging. We've rarely met an expert who is excellent at all of the capabilities listed. Here are some more suggestions to help you keep your approach simple at the same time as achieving impact.

Take a Look at the Relevant Sections of the Guide

- Have a flick through and become familiar with the Guide before deciding which areas to focus on, as there may be some areas for growth that would be extremely useful for you to consider that you have not thought of yet.

Acknowledge your Strengths as well as "Lean in" to Growth areas

- What if you were to grow the areas that you tend to shy away from or that you are resistant to? Would they bring you and the organization more value? You may wish to look at these areas, as often they can bring about significant value. You may also want to consider what strengths you already have that you could potentially "move the needle" on even further and make even more impact in how you work and the results you achieve.

Think – Future Proof?

- As well as considering your immediate growth areas in your current role, we strongly recommend that you focus on the future requirements of your role, the future strategy of the organization and industry you are in, as well as your own personal career plan. This is particularly important in the dynamic and changing world we live in today. Setting yourself up for future success by focusing on the Master Expertship skills that will be required in years to come will stand you in good stead. Use the Guide to assess which of these "enterprise" capabilities will be most important for you in your role and industry for the future.

NOW WHAT?

KEEP IT SIMPLE - CHOOSE 3 GROWTH AREAS'

- We recommend to focus on 3 growth areas at a time to keep it simple and focused. You may want to choose growth areas/skills where you know you will have an opportunity in the future to "practice" the application of. This might be a learning opportunity in an upcoming project or specific meeting. Practising these skills in a "real" situation, will allow you to reach Master expert level more effectively.

Complete your Personal Growth Plan Template

- Once you have chosen the growth areas you would like to commit to you can go ahead and complete your Personal Growth Plan (there is a full description with some examples on how to do this in the next section).

Manager Support

- We talk more about the importance of your Manager's Support in the next section, but we recommend including in your process various "check ins" with your Manager along the way to share, involve, and seek feedback. Knowing your manager is supporting you, as well as keeping yourself accountable to them, will have a big impact on whether you achieve your Plan. Share this Guide with them, and in particular the detail of each of the enterprise capabilities you have selected to focus on, so that they know how best to support you and provide you opportunities and exposure for growth.

Staying Focused – Adopting a Growth Mindset!

- Staying focused on your Personal Growth Plan (PGP) is key! With each new learning opportunity, find some space to review your performance in some way asking, "what could I have done differently, what will I do more of/less of next time?". Remember, there are no mistakes, only feedback and that there is always room for growth!

THE EXPERTSHIP MODEL®

Enterprise Skills   Technical Skills

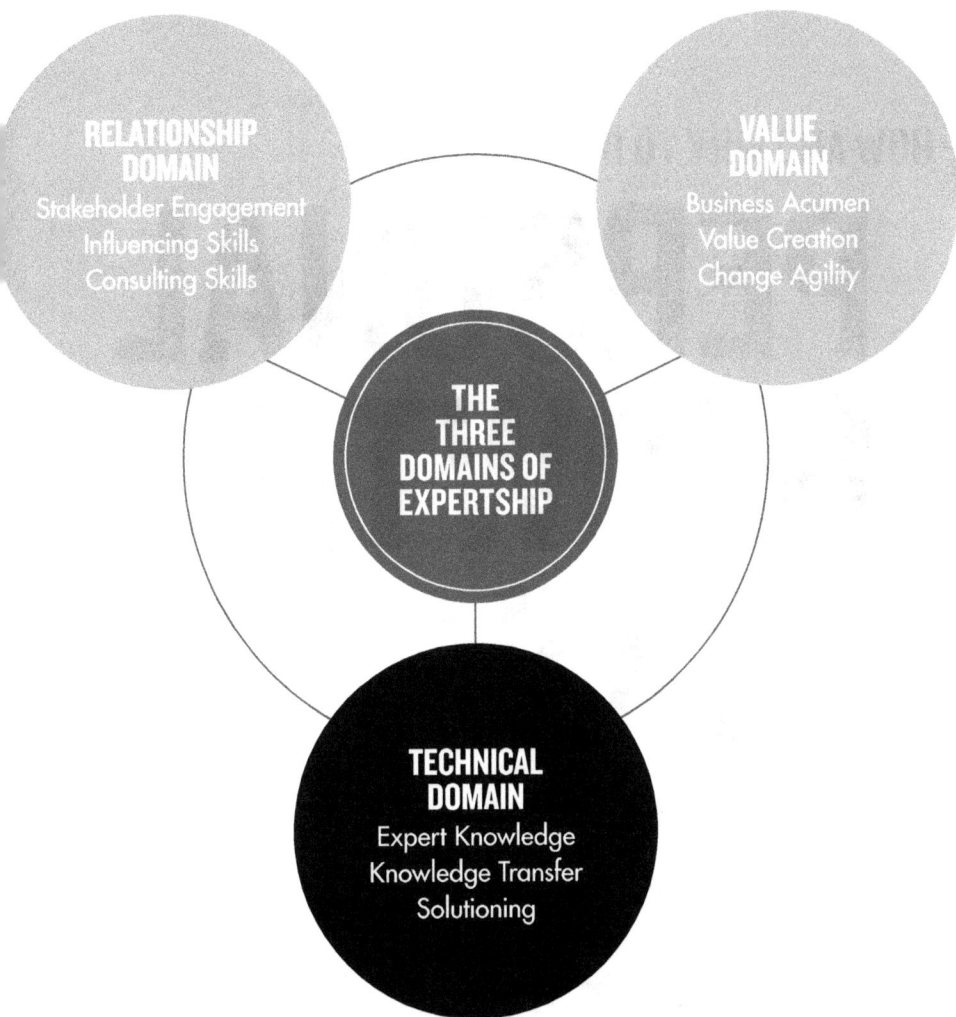

RELATIONSHIP DOMAIN
Stakeholder Engagement
Influencing Skills
Consulting Skills

VALUE DOMAIN
Business Acumen
Value Creation
Change Agility

THE THREE DOMAINS OF EXPERTSHIP

TECHNICAL DOMAIN
Expert Knowledge
Knowledge Transfer
Solutioning

HOW AND WHY TO DEVELOP A
PERSONAL GROWTH PLAN

"THE WHY"

Why Do I Need a
Personal Growth Plan?

In our experience, most experts have a keen learning appetite and often this is a fundamental aspect of keeping their technical and/or professional skills up-to-date. Whilst the various capabilities and certifications in honing their professional and/or technical skills are reasonably obvious, this Expertship Growth Guidebook details additional *enterprise capabilities* that are necessary for experts to be able to add even more value to their organization. Assuming our technical skills are already excellent, this provides a structured approach to take our career and personal brand to the next level.

In the absence of a structured **Personal Growth Plan**, few experts progress beyond the basic and intermediary levels of expertise to reach the level of being a Master Expert. Master Experts are distinguished from Experts and Specialists in that:
- They focus on and deliver compelling real-world outcomes, not merely technical and/or professional inputs
- They are proactive and future-focused
- They are highly engaging and influential

Such capabilities are rarely acquired organically by most experts. In fact, growth in these areas can often feel like a stretch for many of us. Hence, we find that a structured and focused approach to planning is necessary to support the growth of these critical skills and to build on our existing capability.

The approach we take at Expertunity is therefore to help you create and action your **Personal Growth Plan** which will support you in mastering *enterprise capabilities* within these six core areas:

- Influencing and communication skills
- Consulting and solutioning skills
- Stakeholder engagement skills
- Business acumen – understanding market, customers and competitors and the way your organization works
- Value creation -understanding where you can add most value
- Change agility

Creating a Personal Growth Plan is a structured commitment to evolve towards mastery in your role and will allow you to:

- Become aware of the capabilities required for Expertship within these core areas. It allows you to focus on those which will be of most benefit for the business and your own personal growth
- Provide examples of activities that you can undertake now that will advance your development in each of these areas

"THE HOW"

How to Develop a
Personal Growth Plan

Our Personal Growth Plan (PGP) template (p20) will assist you in:
- Thinking through what sorts of target outcomes you'd like to achieve (desired situation)
- Identifying current challenges/issues that you'd like to address/resolve (current situation)
- Identifying the specific steps (activities) you plan to take, tracking progress and keeping yourself accountable

Our recommendation is that you identify 3 "growth opportunities" which will be advantageous to you and your organization. Once you have defined your growth opportunities, complete the Growth Plan Template for the first capability area and then move onto the next ones.

STEP 1: DEFINE YOUR GROWTH OPPORTUNITIES

- Consider which 3 growth areas will provide you and the business the biggest positive impact (you may find it useful to browse the guide to seek ideas)
- Consider your strengths as well as any areas which may be a challenge for you
- Consider any feedback you have received from leaders/stakeholders about your non-technical skills as well measurable feedback you may have received from 360 surveys, project/team reviews, Expertship program if attended, etc.
- "Lean in" to the capability areas that you proactively seek to avoid and explore if it is because you may require some growth.

Questions you might want to consider: What non-technical, future-focused skills are most advantageous across my industry? What feedback have I had around my non-technical skills – what are my strengths to leverage/ challenges? If I could become a master in one area and it would make a huge difference, what would it be?

STEP 2: DEFINE YOUR CURRENT SITUATION

- Describe your current behaviors and the impacts they are having
- Identify and notice where the gaps are between what you are doing and "getting" now and what you would like to be doing and "getting" in the future and consider "why?"
- You might find the "issues you're hoping to prevent or address" section of the guide helpful

Questions you might want to consider: What behaviors of mine are contributing towards those impacts? What do I need to consider doing differently?

STEP 3: DEFINE THE DESIRED SITUATION

The next two boxes on the Personal Growth Plan are to do with the future state you would like to achieve (desired situation).

- Consider the "results you can expect" section of the development guide which may help you identify some positive impacts. Again, you might start there and work your way back to identifying the new behaviors that will in turn produce those positive outcomes.
- Consider what "new" behaviors will bring impact rather than more of the same behaviors

Questions you might want to consider: What is the impact/outcomes you would like to have in this area, what would you see, hear, experience? What new behaviors do you want to adopt? What impact do you think these new behaviors will have?

STEP 4:
ACTIVITIES

This stage refers to the committed steps you will take to achieve your goal.

- List all the actions you will take to progress from current behaviors (and impacts) to desired behaviors (and impacts).
- Identify concrete and specific measures, or signs and symbols of progress, that describe the achievement of your goals such as customer satisfaction measures, completed projects, etc.
- If you don't currently have ways to monitor your progress, consider creating some. Some ideas include regular project tracking meetings or stakeholder engagement questionnaires. You may wish to seek feedback from a trusted colleague, third parties or stakeholders directly about what is working better, and where you potentially still need to focus
- It's vital that you work out each of the steps in enough detail – so that you can subsequently review how to bring to life the actions– ideally, they will each end up as tasks on your To-Do list or appointments in your calendar
- You may find the "actions to take" section in the development guide helpful to you. While we cannot guarantee that the suggestions listed there perfectly and comprehensively apply to your situation, it will give you an idea of the sorts of things that can help you progress towards mastery.

STEP 5:
ACCOUNTABILITY
STRATEGY

This section is designed to help you put in place systems and relationships that assist you in staying on track – holding you accountable to take the actions you are describing above.

- Consider who to make yourself accountable to and how regularly you will report/update them. Commit to what you can practically manage as well as considering the level of support you require.

PERSONAL GROWTH PLAN

IN DETAIL

GROWTH OPPORTUNITY — STEP 1

Consider the 9 core areas and define what kinds of breakthroughs would have the most impact for your own growth and value to the business

DATE: **VERSION:**

CURRENT SITUATION — STEP 2

BEHAVIORS	IMPACTS
What are my future behaviors within the core area	*What are the outcomes I am seeing and the impacts to me and the business? Consider if there are any gaps between the current situation and where you would like to be?*

DESIRED SITUATION — STEP 3

BEHAVIORS	IMPACTS/PAYOFFS
What are my future behaviors that I need to be adopting to have better impacts/payoffs?	*What are the outcomes that I would like to see that are relevant at Master Expertship level?*

STEP 4	ACTIVITY	TIMEFRAME	MEASURE OF SUCCESS
1	*Ensure each column in this section is specific and detailed, including a time by which they will be executed, so that your plan has more chance of being achieved*		
2			
3			

ACCOUNTABILITY STRATEGY — STEP 5

Consider who will be best to be accountable to and decide on how you make yourself accountable

SAMPLE PERSONAL GROWTH PLANS

GROWTH OPPORTUNITY | SAMPLE 1

I want to minimise time spent on urgent/important matters so that I can spend more time working on the strategic aspects of my role in the not urgent/important quadrant.

DATE:	VERSION:

CURRENT SITUATION

BEHAVIORS	IMPACTS
I am reactive and deal with problems as they arise. I classify all tasks as urgent/important and try to do everything at once. Whenever my team members have problems, I solve the problem for them.	*I rarely finish the things I intend to do at the beginning of the day. I spend 95% of my time on 'firefighting' urgent/important tasks as they arise. My attention is constantly split, and the quality of my work is acceptable, but could be improved if I had more time to complete it. Other team members don't have an opportunity to learn how to solve problems and I spend time on tasks I probably don't need to.*

DESIRED SITUATION

BEHAVIORS	IMPACTS/PAYOFFS
I spend 70% of my time on the strategic aspects of my role. I work through my To-Do list in a systematic manner. I trust other members of my team to be able to solve their own challenges with minimal input from me.	*I can produce high quality work for my clients and team. I can finish my day with less rather than more items on my To-Do list. Critical knowledge is distributed to other team members and they are able to develop their knowledge in other areas. I also want to eventually be able to learn the critical aspects of their role as well.*

ACTIVITY | TIMEFRAME | MEASURE OF SUCCESS

	ACTIVITY	TIMEFRAME	MEASURE OF SUCCESS
1	*Plan my tasks so that I understand where I am spending most of my time. Aim to spend 70% of time in the not urgent/important quadrant and 15% of time in urgent/important. Remaining time to be spent on other quadrants.*	*Weekly. Finish transitioning all tasks by end of March 2019.*	*Have a 30 minute time log reflection each week. I am spending 70% of my time (~28hrs) per week on 'big rocks'.*
2	*List out my activities at the beginning of the day and cross off activities as I finish them. Using the extra time I have gained to improve the quality of my work.*	*Daily. Start and continue using this method until end of April 2019.*	*Finishing three 'big rock' activities a day with little to no errors. Placing less importance on 'little rock' activities.*
3	*Instead of solving problems for my team members when they seek my help, I want to coach them through an appropriate solution.*	*Weekly. Until end of June 2019.*	*Practising and using the GROW model once a week. Asking for feedback from my team members.*

ACCOUNTABILITY STRATEGY

I'm going to share my plan with my manager and give my manager updates in our monthly catch ups.

I'm going to share my plan with Sandy who also attended the program with me. We will have fortnightly check-ins with each other to share our successes and challenges, as well as review where we are spending our time.

GROWTH OPPORTUNITY — SAMPLE 2

Adopt more of a results-focused consulting approach so that I can add more strategic value and raise my personal brand

DATE: | **VERSION:**

CURRENT SITUATION

BEHAVIORS	IMPACTS
I tend to respond to requests by giving stakeholders exactly what they ask for – which is not always exactly what they need nor the best use of my time	I believe that I end up branding myself as a low-level doer – technical "inputter" rather than a strategic contributor adding immense value

DESIRED SITUATION

BEHAVIORS	IMPACTS/PAYOFFS
I want to prioritize those requests which have highest biggest impact. I want to flush out relevant impact measures behind each request so that I can design solutions that objectively "move the needle" – and report such business benefits accordingly. I want to educate my stakeholders as to the real value that I can add	I will be seen as "value-adding" strategic partner – and be sought out (early on) by stakeholders for my insightful contributions to the conceptualisation of solutions I will face fewer cost-constraints. I will work on more satisfying assignments – fewer pesky, low-level items (with little to show for the time spent working on them)

	ACTIVITY	TIMEFRAME	MEASURE OF SUCCESS
1	Interview my 3 primary stakeholders and learn proactively of their key headaches and business priorities. Document these as a needs-analysis.	To complete by w/e 14 Sept	Stakeholders' expressed satisfaction with my needs-analysis reports
2	Flesh out my recommendations as to how I can best address their most keenly felt needs and positively impact performance. Including implementation plan and timeline	To complete by w/e 28 Sept	Stakeholders' agreement on a way forward – albeit likely following some back and forth
3	Prior to solution rollout, to agree an evaluation strategy corresponding to each implementation plan. And to subsequently produce a related impact report at the conclusion of each implementation to report benefits.	At the outset and conclusion of each implementation plan	High quality impact reports at the conclusion of each rollout illustrating benefits realised

ACCOUNTABILITY STRATEGY

I'm going to share my plan with my manager and give my manager updates in our monthly catch ups.

I'm going to share my plan with my primary stakeholders too.

WHAT NEXT?

Making It Happen!

In our experience, well-crafted and targeted Growth Plans and the goals they contain are more likely to be seen through to "benefits realization" when:

- There's a compelling reason why they're being done – a valued payoff (a compelling contrast between current and desired impacts)
- The steps are specific enough, comprehensive, realistically timed and measurable
- There is a sense of accountability – progress checks to keep things on track

Manager Support

Once you have developed a draft, we'd recommend you share your action plan with your manager – inviting their input and feedback. Your manager's feedback will not only allow you to finalise your plan and start the process of putting it into action – but you will have, in essence, secured their support and sponsorship to the implementation of your plan. Otherwise you run the risk of any progress that you're making being invisible or seen as a possible unauthorized departure from preferred ways of working – or merely a distraction.

- Do they share your view of the value of the items you've chosen to work on?
- What would they modify?
- Would they recommend any additional steps?
- Are you at risk of over extending yourself?
- Is your timeline realistic and/or aggressive enough?
- Are there any other measures you might consider?

Once you have completed your PGP and presuming that you have shared it (and revised if required) with your manager, we recommend to organize regular check-ins with them to review your progress and seek their support and feedback on key areas.

Your Commitment

Staying focused and remembering the "Why" is important as you grow your skills. Often, we can revert to old patterns and behaviors, or be pulled into old styles of working. Remembering it may take some time to reach Master Expertship level, the trick is to keep reviewing your PGP progress regularly and continue to keep honing your skills and new behaviors until they become more natural. Over time, you will begin to see the positive impacts both for the business and for your own personal career.

MASTERING EXPERTSHIP GROWTH GUIDE

A ROADMAP FOR
ASPIRATIONAL EXPERTS

THE EXPERTSHIP MODEL, or Framework provides us with a new way of thinking about the roles of an expert. The model is a *capability framework* – a description of the skills and knowledge that individuals and organizations need to get things done. When we introduce this model to experts we work with, they often reply "Why didn't someone show me something like this years ago?"

Capability frameworks have existed – for people leaders – for decades. Initially called *competency frameworks*, they were introduced to describe things that organizations were good at. Now they generally describe the behaviors that organizations want their leaders to exhibit, which lead to greater organizational performance.

Technical experts have had *competency frameworks* available to them as well, but these have typically been exclusively used to describe technical competence.

When we undertook a global search for a capability framework for experts that included more than technical competence, much to our surprise, we couldn't find one. So, the Expertship Model, was born, and what is present here is our third iteration.

We are intensely grateful to all of the experts and organizational development folk who have helped us refine it over the past few years. We are sure it can be further improved and look forward to suggestions from the expert community on how to do so.

THE THREE LEVELS OF EXPERTSHIP

Everyone, whatever their line of work, needs a description of what 'good' looks like. This is as true of experts as it is of people leaders. We might argue even more needed.

In sports, there are many measures quoted constantly via statisticians of how well one player's performance compares with another. In many sports there are also different levels of play. In Association Football (soccer), for example, typically teams are organized into different leagues, with the highest performing teams grouped together in the top league, and less well performing teams in lower leagues or divisions (Premier League, Championship, and League One in football in the United Kingdom). These divisions provide an indication of what quality level you are playing at.

Professionals armed with a guide to the capabilities they need to be successful at different levels of performance are able to self-assess or get feedback from colleagues or their manager on the level at which they currently operate. They can then strategically plan to acquire further knowledge and skills that will advance them up the levels to mastery at the highest level.

The Expertship Model has three levels of capability (see Figure 1). These describe the levels at which experts typically operate, and the fourth describes derailing behaviors that can get in the way of experts performing well.

THE THREE LEVELS OF
EXPERTSHIP

Figure 1. The Three Levels of Expertship.

INCREASING VALUE-ADD

SPECIALIST

EXPERT

MASTER EXPERT

RE-RAILING

Master Expert:
- Strategy
- Transformative
- Far Horizon
- Leading, Proactive
- Innovating
- External Focus

Expert:
- Tactical, some strategy
- High value transactional
- Near and mid Horizon
- Following, Reactive, some proactive
- Continuous Improvement
- Department Focus

Specialist:
- Tactical
- Transactional
- Near Horizon
- Following, Reactive
- Task Orientated
- Internal Focus

Re-railing:
- Closed Mindset
- Unresponsive
- Past Horizon
- Disconnected
- Blame orientated
- Self-focus

SPECIALIST

The lowest performance level in the Expertship Model is Specialist. Those we have worked with who profile at this level are often starting out in their expert career or have possibly recently switched roles into a new or adjacent technical domain. They perform very transactional work, usually work that is directed to them by others.

Acquiring knowledge, skills and experience is often the main focus of their attention, learning from mistakes, and shadowing more experienced experts to understand how and why they operate in the way they do. The work specialists execute tends to be highly transactional, focused on making things work properly today, and usually has a strong internal focus. Many specialists work in backroom roles, with little external contact either outside their department or the organization. Specialists are typically learning their trade.

There is nothing inherently wrong with operating at the Specialist level of Expertship – it is simply a stage on the way to greater mastery of the experts' chosen domain expertise. Most experts operating at the Specialist level have a burning ambition to attain a higher level of capability as quickly as possible. It is important to note that traditionally these experts have imagined that this will be achieved purely by the acquisition of more technical expertise. But a scan of the Expertship Model shows them that broader enterprise skills also need to be acquired. This is an insight that usually accelerates their career for reasons we will discuss throughout this book.

EXPERT

The second level of Expertship is the Expert level.

At the expert level, we are describing very capable experts, typically with a great deal of experience, skills and knowledge. The work done by experts at this level is very varied. Plenty of tactical and transactional work still needs to be completed, but occasionally this will be supplemented with some strategic or longer-range work.

Much of the work is still reactive rather than proactive, but greater exposure to colleagues outside the technical department and possibly outside the organization takes place. At the Expert level there will be a focus on continuous improvement and productivity outcomes but the main focus will remain at the departmental rather than what we call the 'Enterprise' level.

The vast majority of experts we have worked with over the last few years have profiled at the Expert level of the Expertship Model. And the vast majority of them felt they were operating at the highest level of Expertship that they could be. For many, it was a rude shock that we had defined a level of Expertship above the Expert level.

MASTER EXPERT

The Master Expert is working on tasks and projects that are strategic rather than tactical, transformational rather than transactional, and far horizon rather than near horizon. Master Experts are proactive and determine their own work and priorities, because the organization sees the value they can add better than any others.

Master Experts operate across the enterprise, with stakeholders at senior levels in the organization and outside of it. They are focused on internal and external customers. Given this description, it will be no surprise to read that they are often at the center of innovation projects, and often play the role of catalyst for change. They dream up the future and get buy-in from the rest of the organization to fund and create it.

WHAT ARE DERAILERS?

A derailer is an expert behavior that gets in the way of our progress. We call them derailers because they are like a train coming off a railway track. We call these behaviors derailers rather than weaknesses, because weaknesses are often viewed as structural and unchangeable.

By comparison, once an expert is aware of the impact a derailing behavior can have on their ability to get things done and deliver value, they can quickly adjust that behavior.

Derailers develop for a range of reasons. They can be a manifestation of a particular skill or talent that is deployed too often. Experts like to remind people of how expert they are, and they tend to do this too often. This can be because they lack awareness or don't understand the negative impact a particular behavior has on their colleagues and other stakeholders. Experts are renowned for 'knowing best' because they are, after all, the experts. This means they often stop listening to alternative points of view, particularly if that point of view is expressed by someone who is not perceived to be an expert in their domain.

Many experts do this unconsciously. In the Expertship Model, we have called out a range of behaviors or habits we see as derailers. We do this at a granular level chapter by chapter throughout this book, but in overview, they can be broadly described as having a closed mindset, being unresponsive to client requests, being focused on the past (what worked before), a lack of connection with critical stakeholders, a blame focus, and being very much focused on their own needs rather than the needs of their department, the wider organization, or external stakeholders such as customers.

AT WHICH LEVEL DO YOU OPERATE?

The work of experts is highly complex. As you might expect, determining what level you operate at as an expert is complex as well. The level you operate at is an average of nine different ratings across the nine capabilities of the Expertship Model.

By way of an example, one expert we worked with, Tony, was without doubt operating at Master Expert level in two areas of the Expertship Model.

When it came to the capability of Expert Knowledge (in the Technical Domain) he had more knowledge, skills and experience in his domain (a specialized field of information technology) than most others, and was *applying* this knowledge strategically and innovatively on a daily basis. He was the go-to person for the enterprise, and no new technology projects were advanced without getting his input and advice. This is the mark of a Master Expert.

The same could be said for the capability of Solutioning. Whenever there was a problem that was out of the ordinary or difficult to solve, Tony was the person everyone went to for solutions. Similarly, when the business was trying to predict future challenges and problems, Tony's input into future solutions was sought out enthusiastically. Tony was known for being able to see round corners when it came to predicting future problems with applications and infrastructure. Again, the mark of a Master Expert.

While it appeared that Tony was on track to be rated Master Expert, it turned out things weren't quite so rosy in the Relationship Domain. Tony took a close look at the behaviors described at Master Expert level under Stakeholder Engagement and considered that he operated at Expert level.

He also noted that he was probably guilty of several derailers when it came to stakeholder engagement (poor external networks and 'difficult to deal with'). Derailing behaviors act as negative marks and if you are deploying two of these derailing behaviors occasionally, then in our assessment tool we would drop you down a level of Expertship performance – which is what Tony did. He concluded that he was operating only at Specialist level when it came to the Stakeholder Engagement capability.

You can see from Tony's example that experts operate at different expert levels in different Expertship capabilities. Your overall rating is an average of all nine capabilities, and most experts need to be operating at Master Expert level in five or more capabilities to achieve the status of being a Master Expert – being the very best expert you can be.

Tony was in many ways quite typical of what we often see. In the past few years we have conducted hundreds of 360 degree multi-rater assessments using the Expertship Model (the feedback tool is called the Expertship360), and many of those assessed score strongly in the technical domain capabilities, but less well in the relationship domain.

THE EXPERTSHIP MODEL

AT A GLANCE

Experts work in highly complex environments, so you might expect the Expertship Model to be reasonably complex as well. The Expertship Model is the basis of our understanding of Expertship, and it includes the Domains of Expertship, the Nine Capabilities and our description of Expert Roles within those.

DOMAINS OF EXPERTSHIP

Within the model itself, the three Domains of Expertship are the highest level of descriptions. These include the Technical Domain, Value Domain and Relationship Domain. The Technical Domain is where most experts are comfortable, and where most learning and development has historically occurred.

NINE CAPABILITIES

The next level down in the Model are the Nine Capabilities (three for each Domain). These are the nine capabilities that we encourage experts to master. The Relationship Domain, for example, has three Capabilities: Stakeholder Engagement, Collaboration, and Personal Impact.

EXPERT ROLES

The Model isn't really helpful until we get into the granular details of what it means, for example, to be a great collaborator. As you will see from the graphic in Figure 3. the next level describes the Expert roles. In the graphic we have highlighted the three roles experts must play if they are to be an effective colleague when it comes to collaboration – a team worker, a communicator, and a diplomat. Figure 3. shows how the above comes together to create our Expertship Model/Framework at a high level.

Figure 2. The Expertship Model at a High Level

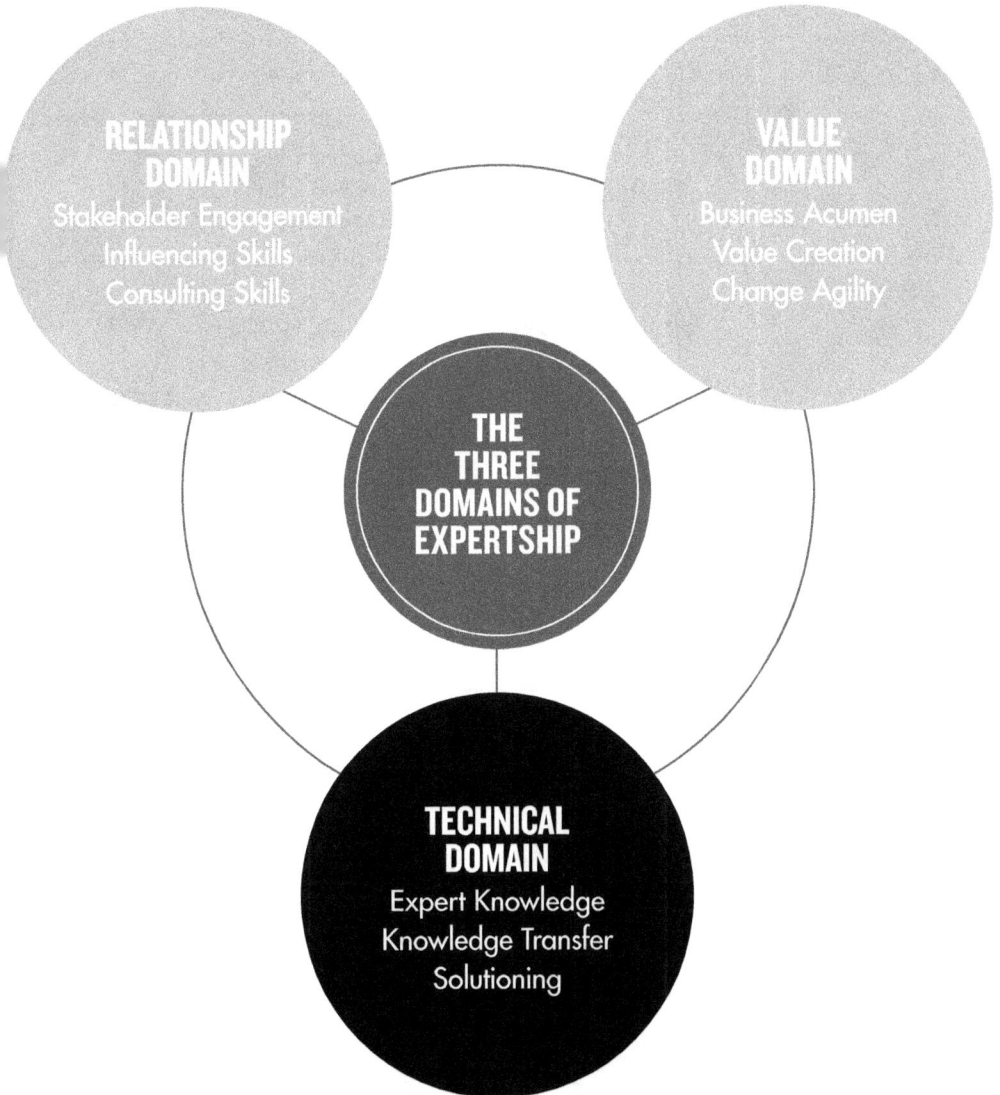

RELATIONSHIP DOMAIN
Stakeholder Engagement
Influencing Skills
Consulting Skills

VALUE DOMAIN
Business Acumen
Value Creation
Change Agility

THE THREE DOMAINS OF EXPERTSHIP

TECHNICAL DOMAIN
Expert Knowledge
Knowledge Transfer
Solutioning

Figure 3. The 27 Roles of Experts, By Capability and Domain

DOMAIN	CAPABILITY	EXPERT ROLE
TECHINICAL	KNOWLEDGE EXPERT	Knowledge Seeker Knowledge Curator Knowledge Generator
	KNOWLEDGE TRANSFER	Knowledge Sharer Knowledge Coach Talent Developer
	SOLUTIONING	Problem Identifier Active Responder Problem Solver
VALUE	MARKET CONTEXT	Organizational Navigator Competitive Analyst Customer Strategist
	VALUE CONTEXT	Operational Value Creator Customer Value Creator Competitive Advantage Creator
	CHANGE IMPACT	Change Supporter Change Catalyst Change Leader
RELATIONSHIP	STAKEHOLDER ENGAGEMENT	Internal Networker External Networker Network Manager
	COLLABORATION	Team Worker Communicator Diplomat
	PERSONAL IMPACT	Positive Influencer Self Aware Adapter Results Driver

THE DOMAINS

IN DETAIL

Now we can take a closer look at the Domains in detail, the capabilities that belong to each domain and the Expert roles within each of those.

Figure 4. The Technical Domain Capabilities and Expert Roles

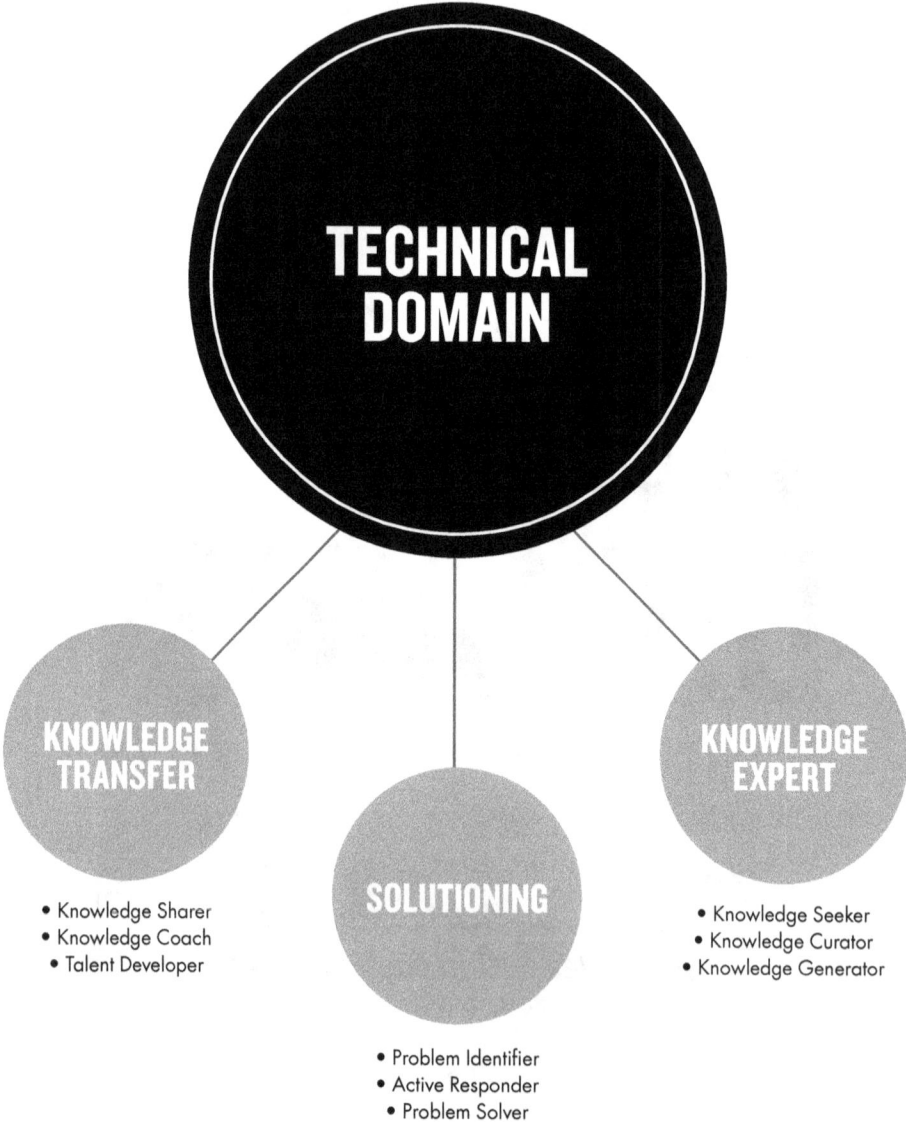

TECHNICAL DOMAIN

KNOWLEDGE TRANSFER

- Knowledge Sharer
- Knowledge Coach
- Talent Developer

SOLUTIONING

- Problem Identifier
- Active Responder
- Problem Solver

KNOWLEDGE EXPERT

- Knowledge Seeker
- Knowledge Curator
- Knowledge Generator

THE TECHNICAL DOMAIN

The Technical Domain covers areas:

- Identifying which key information sources are critical to our success.
- Maintaining and providing access to information sources for key stakeholders across the organization, reducing their dependence on us.
- Understanding how stakeholders wish to consume information and applying relevant versioning, processes and policies.
- Maintaining currency of our expert information, and futurefocus.
- The ability to create new knowledge from the insights we receive from many information sources.

Underpinning all of these is understanding what information is valuable. Many experts have taken a repository approach to their expert knowledge. They regard this repository as the vessel in which all knowledge is stored and asking the organization to come to them to receive wisdom.

Many experts we work with naturally consider this capability one of their strengths. But, while many experts are assessed positively by their peers as having great technical knowledge, they are typically rated less enthusiastically when it comes to making their knowledge accessible to others.

The Technical Domain has three capabilities to be mastered. These are Knowledge Expert, Solutioning, and Knowledge Transfer. See Figure 4.

Knowledge Expert

The capability of Knowledge Expert deals with how experts acquire, retain and grow the deep specialist knowledge and experience they require to do their jobs effectively. This is more complicated and requires more deliberate effort than most experts allocate. If your knowledge is all inside your head, then you are definitely not operating at Master Expert level. Rather, you are a single point of failure risk for your organization and colleagues. The three roles:

- **Knowledge Seeker:** ensuring that the organization has the right knowledge which is current in their technical domain.
- **Knowledge Curator:** making sure that the relevant knowledge is available in meaningful versions to stakeholders and colleagues who need it, and can be easily accessed.
- **Knowledge Generator:** taking existing knowledge and experience and leveraging insights into building new knowledge.

Knowledge Transfer

The capability of Knowledge Transfer deals with developing increased expertise in others to apply specialist knowledge and to facilitate overall increased organizational capability. The three roles:

- **Knowledge Sharer:** ensuring knowledge is disseminated effectively across the organization to relevant parties.
- **Knowledge Coach:** helping colleagues understand and make best use of our specialist knowledge.
- **Talent Developer:** ensuring that both ourselves and colleagues are involved in continuous learning and we actively identify and develop future talent.

Solutioning

The capability of Solutioning deals with the ability of the expert to solve complex technical problems effectively and quickly, via insightful diagnosis, shaping long-term solutions that improve processes and create opportunities. The three roles:

- **Problem Identifier:** understanding where and why problems occur by deploying objective and complex analysis.
- **Active Responder:** responding at an appropriate speed to requests, and getting on the front foot by becoming proactive not reactive, and predicting where requests will come from and why.
- **Problem Solver:** seeing problems through to resolution, and working towards delivering long term solutions.

THE VALUE DOMAIN

The Value Domain covers areas such as:

- Understanding the context in which your organization operates, and the trends and pressures that impact its operation.
- Understanding, where relevant, the competitive environment of your organization; what are your organizations strengths and vulnerabilities in comparison to rival organizations? In the public service sector, this often means identifying alternative services the community substitute for yours, and the impact this might have on your organization.
- Understanding how internal and external customers choose what products and services to buy and consume, and why.
- Being curious and very informed about future trends on all of the above aspects of market context, and thereby being able to operate strategically and long-term in developing plans and initiatives that position your organization for future success.

Underpinning all of these is understanding that information is valuable. Many experts think of themselves as where the knowledge is stored, and that others must come to them to receive wisdom.

A Master Expert will take a publishing approach to their expert knowledge – ensuring access via clever versioning and promotion of the locations where information is stored and available.

The Value Domain has three capabilities to be mastered. These are Market Context, Value Impact, and Change Impact (see Figure 5.)

Market Context

The capability of Market Context deals with the capability of the expert to acquire, retain, refresh and deploy contextual, organizational, competitive and customer knowledge consistently and effectively. The three roles:

- **Organizational Navigator:** understanding and traversing the entire organization, and making contributions at departmental, whole-of-organization and where relevant, global levels.
- **Competitive Analyst:** understanding the competitive landscape from a wide-ranging external business and community perspective.
- **Customer Strategist:** deploying customer centric thinking and action, applied to both internal and external customers, and those who are current, prospective, and future customers.

Value Impact

The capability of Value Impact deals with the capability of the expert to articulate and realize tangible ways of adding commercial or community value, demonstrating an active engagement in improving overall organizational performance. The three roles:

- **Operational Value Creator:** creating real value from incremental technical initiatives to organization-wide efficiencies.
- **Competitive Advantage Creator:** creating real competitive advantage, from incremental change initiatives to breakthrough initiatives that deliver significant advantage over the competition.
- **Customer Value Creator:** creating value for customers and stakeholders, from internal customer value-adds, through to external customer value breakthroughs.

Change Agility

The capability of Change Agility deals with the capability of the expert to act as a change catalyst and lead change initiatives effectively. The three roles:

- **Change Supporter:** champions productive change, avoiding a closed and negative mindset, instead embracing change constructively and positively.
- **Change Catalyst:** generating organizational change initiatives and being the catalyst to making things happen.
- **Change Leader:** leading change initiatives where required, inspiring and managing teams through change.

Figure 5. The Value Domain Capabilities and Expert Roles

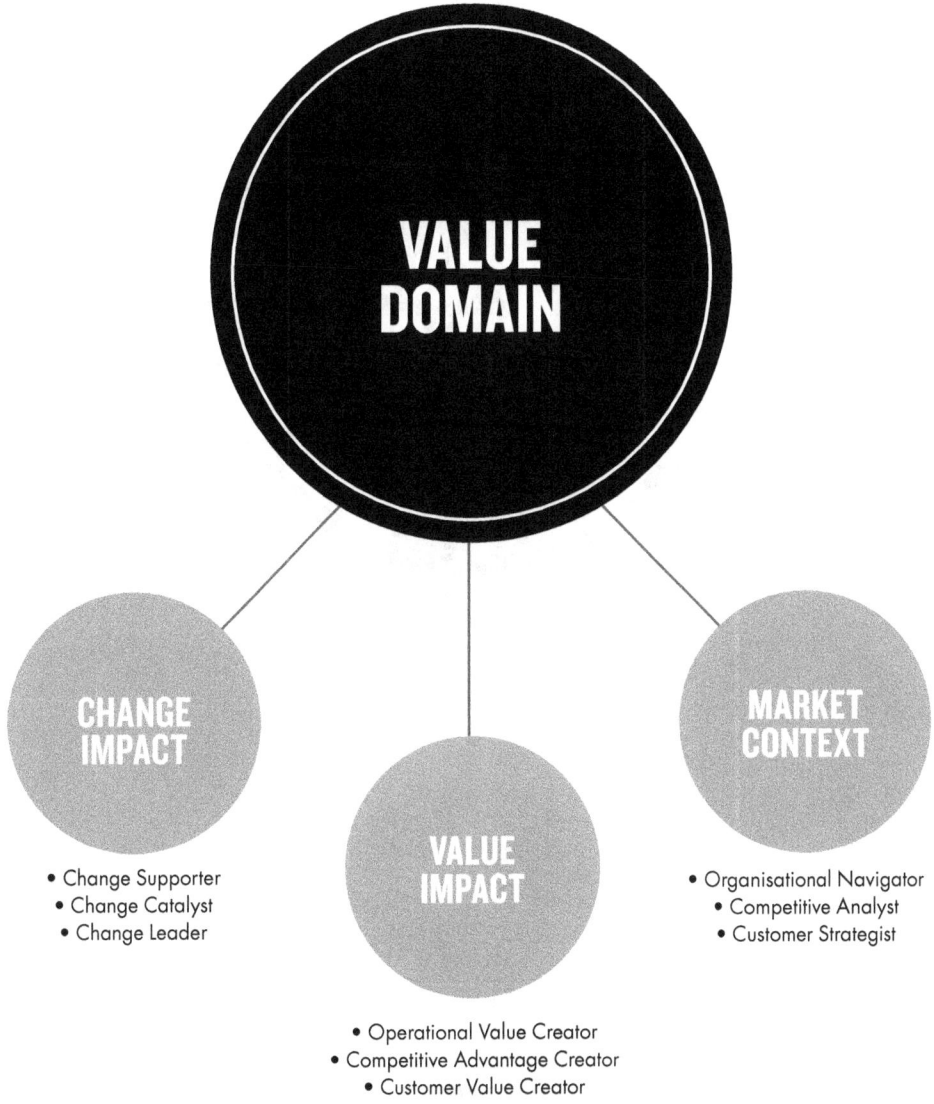

VALUE DOMAIN

CHANGE IMPACT

- Change Supporter
- Change Catalyst
- Change Leader

VALUE IMPACT

- Operational Value Creator
- Competitive Advantage Creator
- Customer Value Creator

MARKET CONTEXT

- Organisational Navigator
- Competitive Analyst
- Customer Strategist

Figure 6. The Relationship Domain Capabilities and Expert Roles

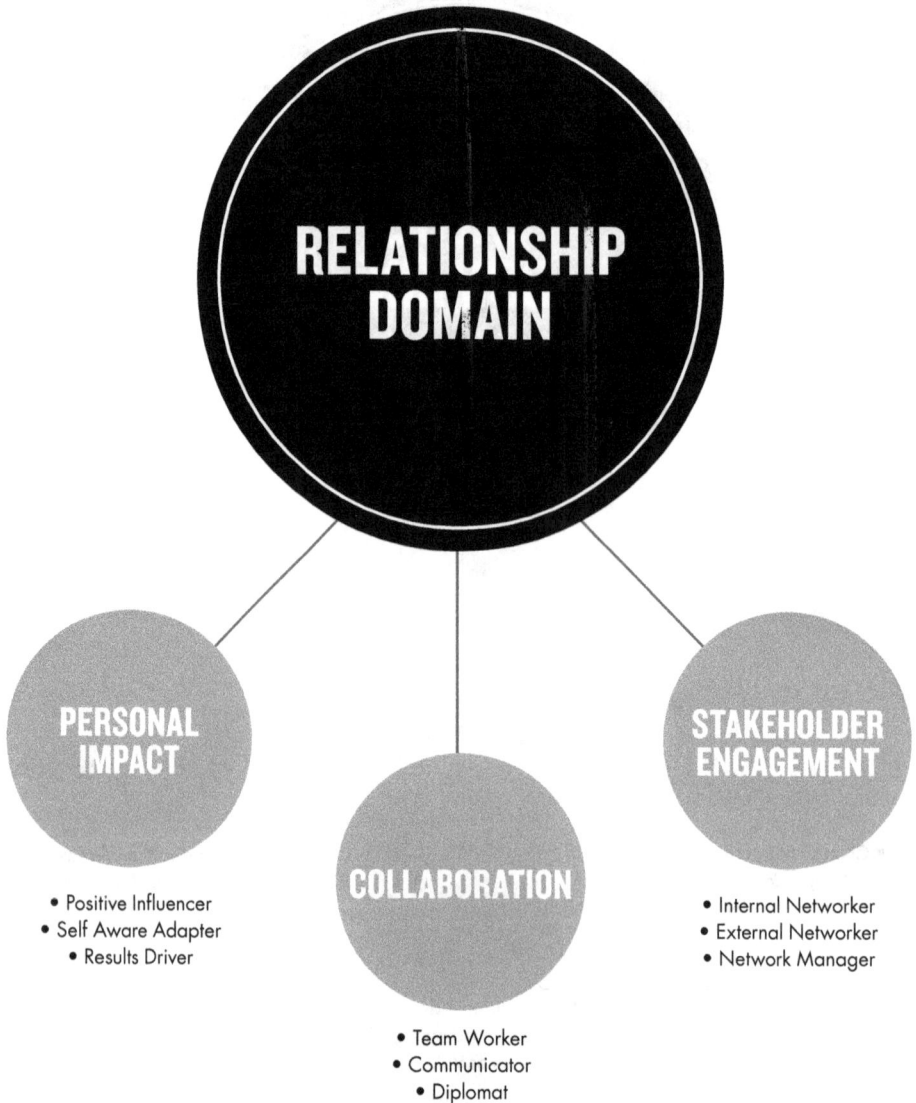

RELATIONSHIP DOMAIN

PERSONAL IMPACT

- Positive Influencer
- Self Aware Adapter
- Results Driver

COLLABORATION

- Team Worker
- Communicator
- Diplomat

STAKEHOLDER ENGAGEMENT

- Internal Networker
- External Networker
- Network Manager

THE RELATIONSHIP DOMAIN

The Relationship Domain covers such areas as:

- Identifying which key relationships and stakeholders are integral to your success.
- Understanding their needs and drivers.
- Engaging and influencing these stakeholders.
- Relationship building and collaboration skills – building trust, listening, courageous conversations, influencing, coaching.

Underpinning all of these is understanding what makes human beings tick.

While many experts in technical roles have had little or no exposure to this kind of material – and have probably been convinced that they are chronically incapable in the relationship domain – in our experience, they learn really fast and have no fundamental disqualifications.

The Relationship Domain has three capabilities to be mastered. These are Stakeholder Engagement, Collaboration, and Personal Impact (see Figure 6)

Stakeholder Engagement

The capability of Stakeholder Engagement deals with how the expert has to build and maintain mutually rewarding stakeholder relationships across a variety of internal and external stakeholder groups. The three roles:

- **Internal Networker:** developing a large and diverse network of stakeholders and colleagues across the organization, both local and global.
- **External Networker:** developing a high-quality external network which is multi-lens and transformational.
- **Network Manager:** effective and efficient at managing and maintaining a large network of colleagues and stakeholders and being proactive and strategic in doing so.

Collaboration

The capability of Collaboration deals with the capability of the expert to act as a valuable, proactive member of their teams, virtual or co-located, taking on a leadership role when required and appropriate. The three roles:

- **Team Worker:** a culturally effective team player, from local and technical to global and organizational.
- **Communicator:** displaying advanced communication skills from rational influence and technical descriptions, to sophisticated influencing skills, with both technical and business fluency.
- **Diplomat:** enabling fast and informed decision making, managing negotiations, all from a facilitative leadership approach, supporting win-win prioritization and outcomes.

Personal Impact

The capability of Personal Impact deals with the ability of the expert to effectively influence others positively, their being self-aware of the impact they have on others, empathetic and adaptive, and the ability to make individual and collective results happen. The three roles:

- **Positive Influencer:** making positive contributions, avoiding cynical and disengaged behavior, instead being inspiring and warm, and demonstrating a can-do attitude.
- **Self Aware Adapter:** aware of their position within the organizational context, very aware of their personal impact on others, and caring.
- **Results Driver:** demonstrating a results orientation, combining advanced prioritization and on-time delivery of agreed outcomes and value.

FINALLY, SOME WORDS OF INSPIRATION

Having worked now with more than one thousand technical experts from a wide range of professions, we've got some good news. Experts in our experience approach capability building with military precision, and in the vast majority of cases make huge strides forward very quickly.

The reason? Because, once you have a roadmap, and clear signposts on how to get from one level of Expertship to another, the actual development of knowledge and skills is the easier part.

Experts, by their very nature, are smart and usually capable of great focus. And, as we have said, in our experience, ambitious – not to be promoted necessarily, or have a fancy title, and certainly not necessary to have an army of people reporting to them – but ambitious to make a bigger difference.

Richard Silberman, an insurance broker told us: "Before I came across Expertship I honestly thought there was something wrong with me. Expertship helped me realize that I am far from being alone. There was nothing wrong with me, I just hadn't learned the right skills."

Lidia Jukic, senior corporate counsel, told us: "I found studying Expertship enabled me to develop a way of thinking that made for a more collaborative environment. I didn't appreciate before the program just how much I have the potential to influence change in the organization. I found Expertship equipped me with the insights and learnings and the tools to become a much more effective member of both the legal team and the overall organization. It helped me refine my skills and become a trusted advisor."

WE ENCOURAGE YOU TO FOLLOW IN THESE FOOTSTEPS.

PART 1

THE
TECHNICAL
DOMAIN

EXPERT KNOWLEDGE

Acquires, retains and grows deep specialist knowledge and experience effectively.

THE THREE EXPERT ROLES OF EXPERT KNOWLEDGE

KNOWLEDGE SEEKER

Ensuring that the organization has the right knowledge which is current in their technical domain.

KNOWLEDGE CURATOR

Making sure that the relevant knowledge is available in meaningful versions to stakeholders and colleagues who need it, and can be easily accessed.

KNOWLEDGE GENERATOR

Taking existing knowledge and experience and leveraging insights into building new knowledge.

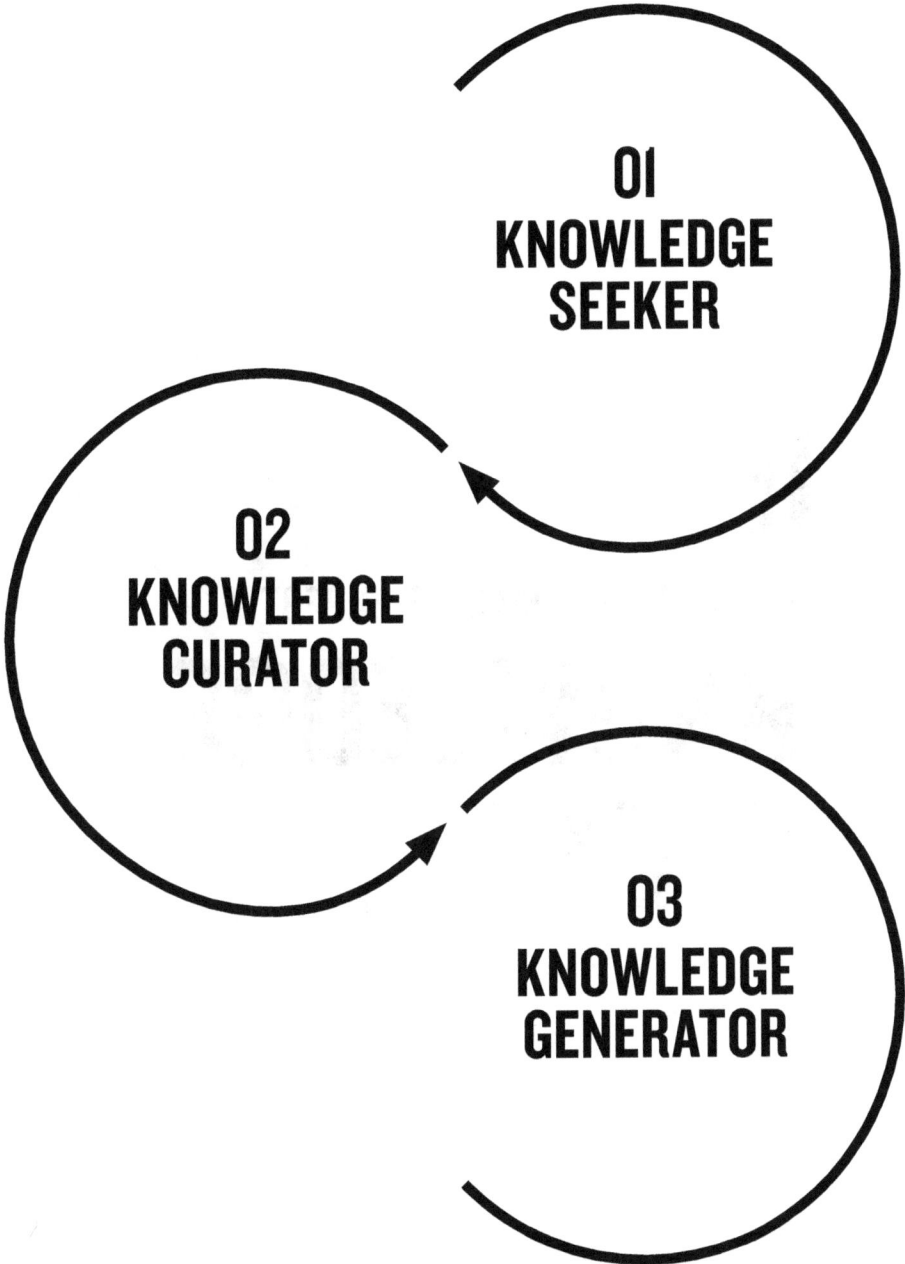

01
KNOWLEDGE
SEEKER

02
KNOWLEDGE
CURATOR

03
KNOWLEDGE
GENERATOR

01

HOW TO BECOME A MASTER EXPERT

KNOWLEDGE SEEKER

CAPABILITY: EXPERT KNOWLEDGE
EXPERT ROLE: KNOWLEDGE SEEKER

MASTER EXPERT	• Continuously updates existing knowledge from traditional and new domain sources, maintaining very high specialist currency. • Continuously challenges existing knowledge assumptions. • Actively seeks new sources of knowledge from domain and non-domain sources.
EXPERT	• Ensures knowledge remains immediately current by continuous engagement in professional development activities. • Rarely challenges well established and accepted assumptions.
SPECIALIST	• Ensures knowledge remains current by periodic participation in professional development. • Relies on well established and accepted assumptions, without challenge.
DERAILING	• Relies on out-of-date knowledge, little time spend on increasing currency. • Dismisses new sources of knowledge as irrelevant. • Completely reliant on narrow domain information sources.

❶ AUDIT CURRENT EXTERNAL KNOWLEDGE SOURCES

Where does your organization get its knowledge from?
Could the process be improved?

CURRENT & FUTURE ISSUES

To ensure an alignment between the knowledge the organization needs and the knowledge it consumes – both currently and for the foreseeable future as too often there is a mismatch. To prevent information sources becoming irrelevant, obsolete, biased, false or superseded by better alternatives.

SUGGESTED ACTIVITY

- Undertake an audit of your current external information sources – industry journals, podcasts, blogs, information feeds and so on. Ask these questions:
  - How current are they?
  - Have any of your long-term trusted information sources been superseded by more up-to-date information feeds?
  - Have adjacent specialist domain sources become more relevant, and are you tracking them appropriately?
  - Do your information sources reflect the future direction of your organization, or the past?
  - Are they sufficiently global in scope?
  - Have new thought leaders emerged that you should be following?

DESIRED SITUATION

The ability to maintain currency is very important and keeps you relevant and valuable. In particular, the ability to articulate how things have changed, and how things will change in the future, makes you a go-to source for many of your stakeholders. They won't come to you if they expect to hear the same old things for the nth time. Master Experts operate globally and across a longer time frame. They are future focussed and one step ahead of the organization's thinking. You can only do this by having a properly thought out set of information sources, possibly with some eclectic choices in there too.

(2) AUDIT CURRENT INTERNAL KNOWLEDGE SOURCES

You and your stakeholders need to know just what information you have available. That way you can ensure it is current and you can work out ways to expand the knowledge base.

CURRENT & FUTURE ISSUES

Prevent a mismatch between who you have talked to historically (and who, of course, may still be relevant) and who you should be talking to now (recent arrivals, recent promotions, head of new project initiatives on culture, transformation, customer centricity, compliance etc.) Prevent internal information sources becoming dated, irrelevant, obsolete, superseded by better alternatives.

SUGGESTED ACTIVITY

- Undertake an audit of your current internal information sources:
    - Are you tuned into 'organization past' or 'organization future?' Are you focused on 'competitors past' or 'competitors future'?
    - What are the major initiatives that the organization is undertaking, and does your network contain key players in those initiatives? Are you focusing on what they are trying to achieve?
    - What are the implications of recent re-organizations?
    - Who appears to have greater responsibility and scope of control now, and who has less?
    - Does this require you to reach out to new people? Are there people who have recently arrived in the business who would be a rich source of competitive and market information (particularly if they have arrived from a competitor), and can you leverage them? New arrivals are always very keen to take meetings that build their network and organizational understanding, so strike as soon as possible.

DESIRED SITUATION

The ability to maintain internal currency, linking your work and prioritization to the changing imperatives, is very important if you are to be seen as current, relevant, and tuned in.
In particular, the ability to foster new relationships as the organization changes, and then leverage these networks for information and influence, is a clear indication of mastery. If you are seen as hanging out only with the 'old gang', your personal brand will suffer, and your influence will wane.

(3)

FUTURE-PROOF
YOUR PRACTICE

Think outside the square. Anticipate what stakeholders will want to know, and plan for those conversations rather than them being a surprise.

CURRENT & FUTURE ISSUES

Think ahead. We all use assumptions to underpin opinions, policies and approaches to the expert work we do, but we face the danger that changing information of market dynamics or indeed customer needs will render these assumptions obsolete or only partially relevant. We want to avoid being asked about issues or requirements that we have not previously considered.

SUGGESTED ACTIVITY

- Undertake a refresh of the evidence-based assumptions you have been using that underpin your practice. Collaborate with others to ask and review whether they are still valid.
- Deliberately go out to test assumptions with stakeholders and customers, undertaking a peer review exercise, and/or doing a scan of what competitors and new entrants to markets may be doing.
- Adopt a mindset to stay open and curious around what can be improved and how your practice will evolve (because to stay relevant change is certain). Consider what new approaches, processes and/or assumptions could be more beneficial.

DESIRED SITUATION

On many occasions as Master Experts we will be asked to explain the thinking behind our policies, procedures and approaches. The ability to reference recent assumption checks and new insights that have been added to our thinking sets us apart from those who stay in their comfort zone. We must guard against being like the frog in the boiling pot of water, unaware of our receding relevance and currency.

4

CHANGE YOUR READING MIX AND KNOWLEDGE ACQUISITION HABITS

The more you read and the wider your knowledge outside your specialty area, the better expert you will become. Don't concentrate only on your specialty.

CURRENT & FUTURE ISSUES

Avoid having a narrow technical focus. You don't want to be perceived as someone people can speak to only about immediate technical issues rather than the broader dynamics and themes impacting the organization.

SUGGESTED ACTIVITY

- The best Master Experts draw from an eclectic mix of information sources outside their specialist domain, a mix they are constantly evolving. This includes interacting with a wide range of people and information sources outside their technical domain and industry.
- Interact with specialists from other domains, geographies and industries. One way of achieving this is to attend industry events that have nothing to do with your specialty. For example, if you are a senior HR executive, attend a digital conference, workshop or webinar. Or if you are in IT, attend a marketing forum to better understand global customer trends.
- Focus on emerging companies and study the waves they are riding to success. When and how will this trend affect your industry? What implications does it have for the work you do today, and the work you may be doing tomorrow?

DESIRED SITUATION

You might be surprised just how useful non-domain knowledge is in your domain. In our experience, it will help you communicate and connect and influence other professions within your organization. It also provides context for longer range thinking. You will be much less likely to hear phrases or trends referenced in meetings that you are unaware of.

02

HOW TO BECOME A MASTER EXPERT

KNOWLEDGE CURATOR

CAPABILITY: EXPERT KNOWLEDGE
EXPERT ROLE: KNOWLEDGE CURATOR

MASTER EXPERT	• Manages a well curated, advanced, comprehensive knowledge bank which is easy to access. • Develops effective versioning of knowledge making our knowledge easy to find and digest by a variety of audiences. • Promotes and models adaptive and innovative usage of existing knowledge and practices, making knowledge actionable and value-creating.
EXPERT	• Has a comprehensive knowledge bank of both common and uncommon concepts, practices and approaches. • Systematic usage of exiting knowledge and practices.
SPECIALIST	• Sound understanding of common concepts, practices and approaches. • Shows developing use and application of knowledge.
DERAILING	• Significant knowledge acquisition still required. • Inconsistent and arbitrary storage of knowledge. • No consideration given to the information needs of others, particularly those outside their technical domain.

(5) UNDERTAKE A STAKEHOLDER ACCESS TEST

Can your key stakeholders find what they need from you, and can you quickly find what you are asked for? Is information saved in places only you can navigate?

CURRENT & FUTURE ISSUES

You have a broad range of knowledge, insights and tools that you have built over time to assist your stakeholders and build their capability to help themselves. But none of this work and none of these resources are valuable unless your stakeholders can find this information without your assistance. Common mistakes include experts filing and organising information from their expert technical areas, rather than asking themselves what their stakeholders are searching for. Are the files and tools and repositories listed in such a way that stakeholders will understand the value of the resources? You do not want to be constantly interrupted by stakeholders asking you for documents that they could – if properly organized – find themselves. If you are serving a multinational stakeholder group operating in different time zones, you want to avoid delay at their end responding to issues because they are waiting for you to wake up in your time zone to ask you.

SUGGESTED ACTIVITY

- The ultimate test is to ask stakeholders what they need and why. Consider whether they can easily find it. Undertake a stakeholder access test.
- Every time you are asked to supply a document or resource, ask yourself why they couldn't find it – or take the time to find it – themselves. What barriers (real or imagined) are in the way of finding the information?
- What artefacts or techniques could you deploy to make finding valuable information in your domain easier for those who need it? For example, would a Frequently Asked Questions document assist in helping people understand how to find what they are looking for? How about a wiki that is not technical, but customer focused?
- Consider what a curator actually does, and why this role is important. Understand that you hold information on behalf of a wider community. Great curation allows people to be exposed to the information, ideas, processes and procedures they need – when they need it.

DESIRED SITUATION

Saving time. Great curation leads to greater self-reliance and autonomy, and your stakeholders depending on you less, particularly those you may perceive to be high maintenance. Better brand. In the expert world, Customer centricity is the ability to enable our stakeholders (customers) to find what they are looking for, and to add value, quickly and easily. You need to know ahead of time what they might ask for and have it ready for them when they do. This is Master Expertship personified!

6 DEVELOP AUDIENCE VERSIONS OF YOUR KNOWLEDGE

Developing logical and easy to digest briefings for different audiences (technical and non-technical) is an important part of sharing our knowledge in a truly accessible way.

CURRENT & FUTURE ISSUES

Minimize time consuming requests for information, or explanations of technically dense documents by a variety of less technical stakeholders. Improve understanding of the importance of key issues by senior non-technical stakeholders in the organization through the use of plain and accessible language.

SUGGESTED ACTIVITY

- Categorize your audiences in terms of the type of information they want and can easily consume. Then develop multiple versions and make these available to relevant audiences. Test existing information sources for their digestibility by audiences. Would versioning documents for specific audiences (technical and non-technical) assist in clarity and the effective and efficient curation of knowledge?
- Consider whether meaning and implications are clearly enunciated in your documentation. For example, the implications of a technical change in compliance rules might be blindingly obvious to you (the expert), but not be at all to a non-technical audience.
- Undertake a jargon check. It might not be jargon to you, but you'll be surprised how much of your technical language that you take for granted is like a different language to other non-technical parts of the business. Where necessary, develop glossaries that help non-technical stakeholders divine the meaning of particular phrases and terminology. Using technical jargon doesn't demonstrate how clever you are, it demonstrates how out of touch with the rest of the organization you are.

DESIRED SITUATION

Better informed stakeholders who have greater understanding of the issues and challenges you are facing (and why). Quicker resolution of issues, requests, funding etc., because the wider organization understands the import of changes in rules, approaches, suppliers, etc. More meetings about what to do about something (action!) rather than meetings consumed with trying to understand the issues at hand.

7

DEPLOY YOUR KNOWLEDGE CREATIVELY

Bringing your knowledge to life by using multimedia, stories, case studies, videos, quizzes, challenges, etc. Master Expert curation means you take accessibility and interest to a new level by deploying the information and knowledge in many forms.

CURRENT & FUTURE ISSUES

Better targeted knowledge. It is easy to spend lots of time producing insightful information for the business but presenting it in such a way that it doesn't reach its target audience. Greater impact. The wider organization is oblivious of critical impacts and changes happening in your domain, because the way in which it is communicated is opaque at best or impenetrable at worst. Less is more. Don't make the fatal mistake of thinking that the more information we communicate to stakeholders the better. It isn't. First level communication should be to get attention and make a single simple point. If they are then engaged with the message, they'll seek more from you.

SUGGESTED ACTIVITY

- The marketing department may be able to help, but any Self-respecting Master Expert will take some time to think about how key audiences would best like to consume information. Leveraging the knowledge they have about what keeps their stakeholders awake at night.
- Case studies are particularly useful for bringing to life the implication of not following a particular policy or procedure. Our favourite example was a case study of a mid-ranking executive who used a non-encrypted USB drive in her laptop and was unable to send emails for a week. She didn't follow the basic security guidelines. It makes the end users really think about the implications of not following a policy far more effectively than a list of reasons that no one will read.
- Simplify, simplify, simplify and focus, focus, focus. Make sure that the essential information and impacts are clearly communicated, and don't bog down communications with over-communication. If they need more information they can go to the next level of detail and you can help them navigate to that document or process.

DESIRED SITUATION

Your newsletters and other communications are actually opened, because you have built a brand of communicating effectively and only when necessary. Communications from you are generally easy to consume and useful, and they add value.

03

HOW TO BECOME A MASTER EXPERT

KNOWLEDGE GENERATOR

CAPABILITY: EXPERT KNOWLEDGE
EXPERT ROLE: KNOWLEDGE GENERATOR

MASTER EXPERT	• At the vanguard of industry breakthroughs—introducing innovative solutions and seeking to operate at next practice. • Actively contributes to the generation of new knowledge; anticipating long term future knowledge requirements and makes suitable and timely provisions. • Drives an environment that stimulates others to engage with knowledge generation.
EXPERT	• Seeks and adopts new effective knowledge management practices—seeks to operate at best practice. • Anticipates near future requirements, and makes suitable and timely provisions. • Creates an environment for others to engage with.
SPECIALIST	• Demonstrates sound knowledge and adherence to existing knowledge management practices.
DERAILING	• Does not contribute to knowledge generation. • Resists documenting any new practices. • Fails to anticipate or embrace future needs or developments.

8 CREATE A 'BEST AND NEXT PRACTICE' PLAN

As experts we hope we are operating at best practice level in our technical domain. However, to get to Master Expert level, we need to be focused on getting to the next level of expertise, as quickly as possible. To do this we need a deliberate and documented plan.

CURRENT & FUTURE ISSUES

If you are stuck on best practice you will never become a recognised Master Expert. You will be destined to spend your time catching up with people who are constantly redefining what best practice is. Best practice makes you a competent expert, but you are not contributing new value to your organization. "If you always do what you always did, you will always get what you have always got" – Albert Einstein. For organizations to really stand out, they need to be growing, changing and evolving, even more quickly now than ever before. If you can't help them do this, you could be left behind.

SUGGESTED ACTIVITY

When considering best practice and compliance requirements, always remain outcome/solution focused and balance the approach to ensure you deliver exceptional results as well as meeting best practice standards.

- With permission and where relevant, leverage existing work that has been completed so that you can focus on adding value in other ways – such as contributing new ideas for further improvement or to evolve projects.
- Collaborate with others and seek their thoughts and ideas (including stakeholders) around which parts of best practice approaches are the most effective/important and on adopting those and leaving the rest.
- Conduct a strategic review on where you or your team are spending most of your time and look at ways that you can improve the processes that are less efficient so that you can spend more time on adding real value in your practice.
- Take calculated risks and try new things when it is safe and appropriate to do so. Communicate that you are doing this to your teams and stakeholders and the reasons why. Don't be afraid of failure, always take the learnings forward, even with ideas that don't work.
- When new approaches or ideas work, document and share so that others can also receive the benefit.
- Work with, rather than against other expert competitors, particularly in the same industry. By sharing, collaborating and testing new things together, you will raise the collective bar.

DESIRED SITUATION

To be recognised for trying new things and implementing effective practices that you, your teams and organization will all benefit from. To adopt a mindset of being "curious" around how to improve and evolve, whether that be systems, processes, approaches or how to engage.

9

OBSESSIVELY RESEARCH CUSTOMER, STAKEHOLDER AND ORGANIZATIONAL NEEDS

We can't create new knowledge or insights unless we are constantly aware of the way our services are being consumed. We need to know how they are being consumed now, and how they will be consumed in the future. New insights will come from researching this.

CURRENT & FUTURE ISSUES

Doing it the way we've always done it will not be good enough for long. There is always someone out there designing a better, faster, more efficient or more refined way of doing things and delivering services. Being sidelined by major changes in our domain knowledge area which we didn't see coming. It is too easy to be asleep at the wheel.

SUGGESTED ACTIVITY

- Access mundane but insight-rich data. Understand what regular information is collected by the organization that might be useful to you in gaining insights about current and future trends. An example of a typically opaque information source that is rich in insight is customer complaints data. What are customers complaining about and why? Another is analyzing enquiries submitted to your organization's website or social media accounts. What are customers asking and why?
- Subscribe to macroeconomic newsletters. The daily news and most news on the web simply report what people are saying or doing today. What real innovators need is access to longer range macroeconomic insights and data that tells the longer story.
- Befriend the marketing department. When it comes to customer insights, your marketing team should be a strong source of excellent data about the changing nature of customer requirements, needs and attitudes. If they are not, beware! You are probably in an organization that is about to be overtaken by more informed competitors. Marketing will have internal news feeds they share – get on them.
- Turn your travel time into research time. Subscribe to broader economic trend or industry trend podcasts, from both inside and outside your industry. Turn otherwise dead time into research time.
- Deploy advanced future thinking. Get ready to spend plenty of protected time thinking about 'what if' scenarios built on things you have learned. How would this trend play out in my industry or organization or technical domain? What might I do to benefit from the trend? How might it negatively affect my work and my team's?

DESIRED SITUATION

You'll benefit from greater business and community situational awareness. You'll understand more about what's going on in your geography, industry, organization and competitors. You'll understand what's coming down the track and have more time to plan for it. You'll understand impacts on your environment quicker than others around you, which will make you look smart because you will provide first mover advantage. You'll come across as someone with broader wisdom, knowledge and insights rather than just the tech person who runs the comms network.

10 BECOME A STUDENT OF BREAKOUT INNOVATION COMPANIES

Breakout companies – those doing new things – have often spotted a trend or consumer behaviour change that is coming to a workplace near us. They are a great source of knowledge generation

CURRENT & FUTURE ISSUES

Innovation rarely occurs in silos. Whether it is siloed thinking in your department, or your division, or your organization or your industry, without going beyond these familiar territories, we will likely be guilty of siloed thinking. We hope to be across new and changing customer habits, business models and service models so that we can contemplate how to bring these innovations into our knowledge realms.

SUGGESTED ACTIVITY

- Track breakout growth companies and understand how and why they have managed to create new value for customers. Contemplate how these principles might be applied in your organization.
- Track how departments like yours in other industries are tackling problems and increasing productivity - might the changes they are making be applied within your organization?
- Track down and read biographies of corporate and government leaders who have changed the game, and understand how they did it; ask, are similar possibilities available to you and your colleagues?

DESIRED SITUATION

You'll benefit from having a broader knowledge and experience base across the spectrum of innovation companies and ideas. The more you read more broadly, the more you'll see trends and connections, and as a consequence, the more you'll be able to see new value propositions and innovative service and productivity gains for your organization. Your personal brand will evolve from technical guru to business thinker.

II

CHAMPION A ROBUST REVIEW PROCESS WHICH CREATES A KNOWLEDGE GENERATION CULTURE

There are hundreds of small lessons available to us just by closely looking at what we just did and how effective it was. Are we leveraging this?

CURRENT & FUTURE ISSUES

We hope to avoid being so busy completing work that we never stop to consider how effective the work was, whether it achieved the value imagined when briefed in, and whether we could have executed the project or task more effectively with hindsight. We seek to learn from reviews which make us better next time.

SUGGESTED ACTIVITY

- Insist on reviews, no matter how busy we are, on projects that are completed. Incorporate with celebrations that projects have been finished reviews that start with the question "what did we learn?" and finish with the question "if we had our time again, what would we do differently?"
- Conducting such reviews builds a culture that is consistently looking for small productivity wins, and a culture where everyone on the team is taking ownership of innovative improvement.
- Invite participants in these reviews to arrive ready to contribute one thing that went really well on the project, and at least one thing that could have been done better / faster / cheaper / more effectively. As this culture builds, these reviews will become more and more valuable.

DESIRED SITUATION

While remembering to celebrate work being completed (and perhaps great work), you are contributing to a culture that is creatively and innovatively restless. This makes knowledge generation a team sport, with a constant stream of suggested improvements for conducting work next time.

KNOWLEDGE TRANSFER

Develops increased expertise in others to apply specialist knowledge and to facilitate overall increased organizational capability.

THE THREE EXPERT ROLES OF KNOWLEDGE TRANSFER

KNOWLEDGE SHARER

Ensuring knowledge is disseminated effectively across the organization to relevant parties.

KNOWLEDGE COACH

Helping colleagues understand and make best use of our specialist knowledge.

TALENT DEVELOPER

Ensuring that both ourselves and colleagues are involved in continuous learning and we actively identify and develop future talent.

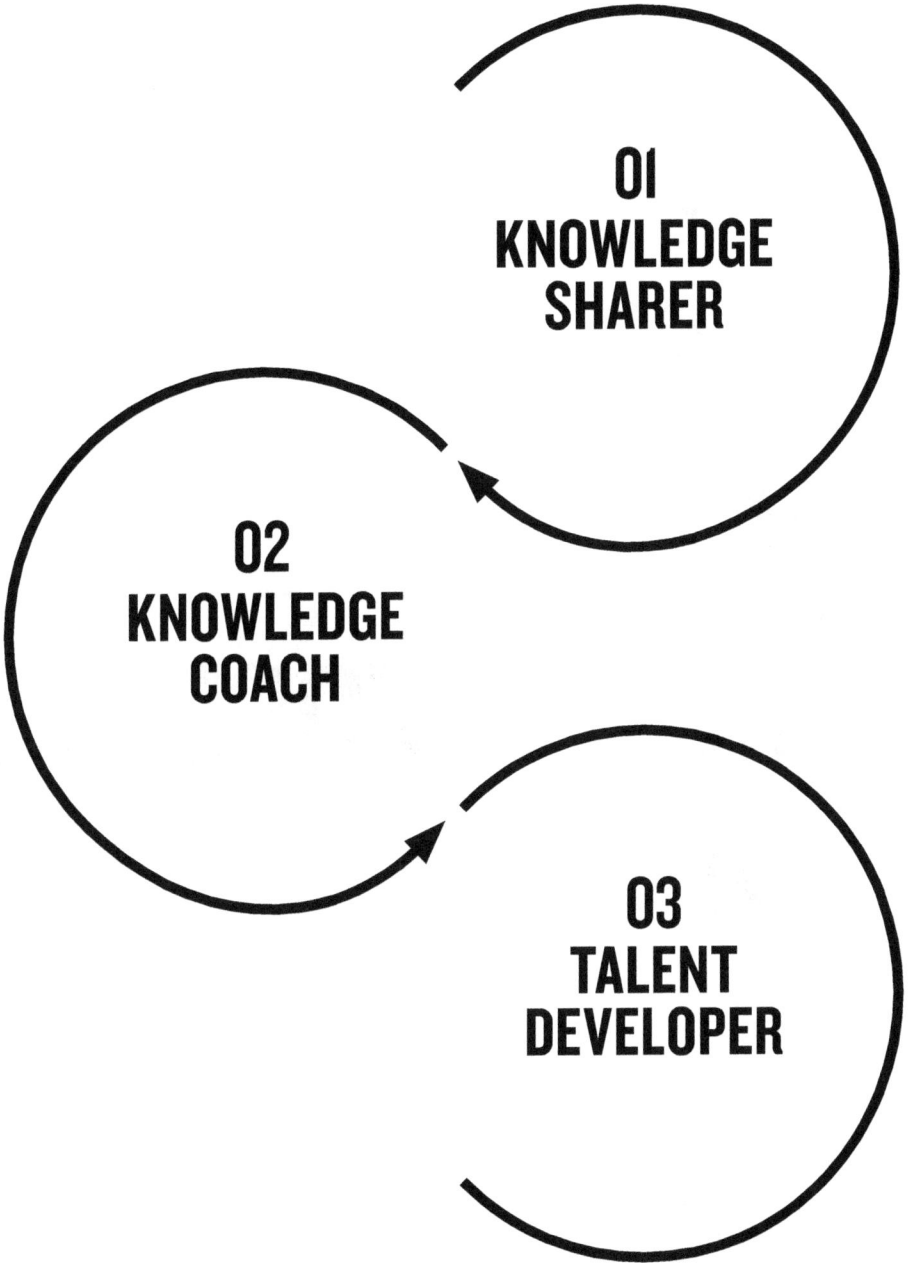

01
KNOWLEDGE
SHARER

02
KNOWLEDGE
COACH

03
TALENT
DEVELOPER

01

HOW TO BECOME A MASTER EXPERT

KNOWLEDGE SHARER

CAPABILITY: KNOWLEDGE TRANSFER
EXPERT ROLE: KNOWLEDGE SHARER

MASTER EXPERT	• Actively champions and role models a culture of knowledge sharing within the organization. • Actively and freely shares all current and relevant information in order to empower others and enable self reliance. • Motivates very broad network to participate in and deploy learning, and regularly checks-in on deployment. • Deploys a deliberate and consistent promotional effort to leverage our knowledge repository to make it front of mind for those who need it.
EXPERT	• Understands the importance of sharing knowledge, but doesn't make it a priority. • Communicates current and relevant information on a 'need to know' basis. • Motivates immediate network to participate in and deploy learning. • Contributes to the knowledge repository.
SPECIALIST	• Is mostly a recipient of knowledge sharing activities. • Occasionally assists reactively, with sharing knowledge across the organisation.
DERAILING	• Provides information to others, but only when requested to do so; tends to hold information close. • Resistant to handing over knowledge, conceals and withholds vital information.

(12) INSTITUTIONALIZE INCIDENTAL LEARNING

Encouraging teams of people to learn and create new knowledge is very much part of the role of Master Expert. We produce new knowledge and insights ourselves, but it is our ability to motivate a wide group around us to also do so that makes us a knowledge champion.

CURRENT & FUTURE ISSUES

The biggest breakthroughs in innovation come from comparatively new insights being combined into a new product or service. This means that no matter how good we are as individual experts, we're unlikely to make breakthroughs on our own. Getting access to broader learning is imperative. Competitive advantage is all about constantly seeking to do things in a more productive way. This is a team sport, and our roles as Master Experts in encouraging team efforts are critical. If the senior experts aren't banging the drum, then more junior experts will follow them into complacency.

SUGGESTED ACTIVITY

- Institute 'Share and Tells'. Incidental learning happens for experts almost every day, but because we are so busy executing tasks or fixing problems, we never have time to share them. Multiplied, this means a team never gets to learn what everyone else on the team has learned.
- We need to create protected time to devote to sharing and learning. In our business we have orange days, days in which all of our consultants are not allowed to service clients, but have to be available to participate in Share and Tell sessions, where what we have learned over the past couple of months is shared among the group and discussed. You might not want a physical meeting but ask people to contribute to a more structured communication such as a newsletter. Actually talking about things leads to much greater probing of the reasons why things are changing, which leads to great insights.
- Seek feedback every moment of every day. Become the person who asks "what did you learn today?" Become the person who asks stakeholders "how could we have done this better for you?". Be the person who asks every stakeholder what's changed and why at every opportunity.

DESIRED SITUATION

You will be building innovative capability across the teams in which you operate. You will be building your brand as a restless innovator who constantly seeks to understand what is changing and why and the threats and opportunities these changes create. You'll be learning new insights and knowledge much more regularly that are likely to feed into greater effectiveness in the provision of the value you offer your organization.

13 BECOME GOOD AT PRESENTING YOUR EXPERTISE TO DIVERSE GROUPS

The ability to explain in simple but meaningful terms to diverse groups of stakeholders is a critical skill of a Master Expert.

CURRENT & FUTURE ISSUES

Avoiding the 'technical bore' label, where you talk in impenetrable jargon, aiming to prove how smart and advanced you are. This is not effective communication. It only turns an audience off and presents a personal brand that discourages people to connect and collaborate. We wish to avoid others not understanding or appreciating the work you and your team do, and how you add and maintain value.

SUGGESTED ACTIVITY

- Study how the best presenters build and then deliver their presentations.
- Attend conferences and study which speakers get good reviews and strong audience attention and respect, and which ones don't – and why.
- Research your audience. Make sure you know what they are interested and not interested in, what keeps them awake at night, and what success looks like for them. Take all of these into account in planning the delivery, structure and content of your presentation.
- Start accepting invitations to present at small groups, and then build up to larger groups. Test your content – what worked for certain audiences, and what didn't? Use an iterative process to refine your messaging, content and delivery.
- Get videos of yourself presenting and take a look at how you are experienced by the audience. This may be a bit scary, but it is a very valuable way to eliminate silly little habits which detract from your message.
- Undertake a public speaking course. However, we only suggest this if you then take the big decision to accept invites and put the skills into immediate action – practice makes perfect.

DESIRED SITUATION

You can to quickly improve the impact of your presentations and start to get positive feedback. You will gradually increase the influence you have with other stakeholder groups as you get to understand them more and customize your content and delivery to match their interests.

(14) CREATE A VERSIONING STRATEGY

As experts, we operate in a highly complex web of stakeholder and projects groups. Their information needs are different, and we have to have a sensible strategy to deal with these differences.

CURRENT & FUTURE ISSUES

Production of content and resources, reference material and news feeds which are generic, and don't meet anyone's needs precisely. We are seeking to ensure that our various stakeholder groups can easily find and consume the information they need from us.

SUGGESTED ACTIVITY

- Build a map of different stakeholder groups and consider their varied information needs. How would they like information presented? What language would they be comfortable with? What level of detail do they need? What sort of search terms would they use to find the content you are providing (as opposed to your very technical descriptions)?
- Undertake a discovery process – research – to see what type of material each group consumes.
- Undertake testing – produce a document, resource or guide and test the design and version with the target group, and other groups, to help you discern the subtle differences that impact how digestible and useful the content is to your various stakeholder groups.
- Develop rules for versions for each stakeholder group and templates that reflect these.
- Gradually morph existing content into these versions, carefully labelling them so the right group consumes the right material. Create all new content along these lines.
- Note: this sounds like a great deal of work, but often the differences require us to cut down length and complexity as our stakeholders become more removed from our technical domain, and this is less time consuming than we might imagine. In some instances, stakeholder groups need quite different material – for example, the wider organization reacts best to case studies and stories rather than in-depth technical descriptions which might be favoured by our technical cohort.

DESIRED SITUATION

Whether senior executives or colleagues from our technical cohort, we are providing carefully customised and refined resources that are easy to find and easy to consume for our various conversation groups.

15 CREATE A DISTRIBUTION STRATEGY

There is little point in producing great content and insights if the information doesn't reach the target audience in a way in which they can easily and in a timely fashion consume it. Distrbution is often overlooked but a crucially important aspect of knowledge sharing.

CURRENT & FUTURE ISSUES

We wish to avoid an incoherent or sporadic approach to knowledge dissemination, or one that assumes one approach suits all stakeholder groups. We want to make sure that our stakeholders are consistently reminded about the expertise available to them so that they can find it when they need it.

SUGGESTED ACTIVITY

- Develop a specific plan to address the information needs of each stakeholder group. This will include frequency of contact, communication channel (webinars, newsletters, alerts, podcasts etc) settings for each group, which are likely to vary.
- Schedule the creation of new material and content so that there is consistent reach out to stakeholder groups, regardless of how busy you are.
- Ensure you have asked stakeholder groups which communication/ distribution channel they prefer.
- Create metrics and use platforms that enable you to assess the number of opens, click-through's etc, from your communication so you can see which content is being accessed and which is not; this enables you to amend your approach and build effectiveness, and at the same time not waste people's time by sending them information they never open.

DESIRED SITUATION

Consistent high-quality communications, carefully crafted for each audience, building a positive brand reputation for your knowledge practice.

02

HOW TO BECOME A MASTER EXPERT

KNOWLEDGE COACH

CAPABILITY: KNOWLEDGE TRANSFER
EXPERT ROLE: KNOWLEDGE COACH

MASTER EXPERT	• Always deploys a question based, collaborative coaching style. • Shares the 'why' to ensure others understand the business value. • Proactively provides information sessions about domain knowledge to colleagues from outside the technical domain, to assist with their understanding. • Is actively sought out by a wide range of stakeholders to provide highly engaging, pragmatic, and effective training/presentations.
EXPERT	• Deploys a combination of 'asking' and 'telling' when coaching on technical knowledge to develop other technical experts. • Occasionally provides pragmatic and effective training/ presentations, particularly to less qualified technical colleagues; sharing the 'how' to support capability development.
SPECIALIST	• Interacts from a learning perspective almost exclusively in the technical domain with technical colleagues. • Shares the 'what' (i.e., the tasks and goals) when training others.
DERAILING	• Deploys a directive, telling training style. • Presentations are unengaging and lead to few effective learning outcomes.

16 ADOPT A COACHING APPROACH TO KNOWLEDGE AND SKILLS DISSEMINATION

The only way to find time to be more strategic and operate at a Master Expert level is to be a brilliantly effective delegator. Which means we need to take the step from having a "tell" strategy to an "ask" strategy.

CURRENT & FUTURE ISSUES

Delegate and coach. If we are constantly showing colleagues how to do tasks, or doing them ourselves, we are building dependency on our expertise. This means we are always in demand to do junior tasks, and we are unable to concentrate on creating strategic value. Our ability to delegate is dependent on our ability to coach colleagues to be as competent – or even more so – than we are on the tasks we delegate. We want to avoid having to tell people how to do things multiple times, or at least minimize the time to successful delegation. A coaching approach helps colleagues learn faster.

SUGGESTED ACTIVITY

- Adopt the first rule of coaching in your coaching conversations – 'ask don't tell'. Convert the statements you want to make into questions that lead your colleagues to the answer. This also makes the learning far more memorable.
- Adopt the second rule of coaching in your coaching conversations – 'listen intently'. By doing so you'll discern what your colleagues understand and what they do not. You'll also understand what they are finding difficult.
- Use a situational learning approach – think of typical problems that you have to solve. You want to coach colleagues to be able to solve them instead of having to do it yourself. Ask them to consider how they would initially try and solve the problem.
- This questioning technique, with intent listening and your experience of how these problems are usually solved, will help your colleagues move towards a solution. A handy technique is to ask them to think of three approaches, and consider the pros and cons of each, and then suggest which one they would choose. This provides you with a framework for a rich conversation and exploration of the implications of taking one approach over another.
- Focus on the 'why', not just the 'what' and the 'how' in your coaching sessions. If your colleagues understand why one approach is taken rather than another, they are more likely to be able to apply the skills more broadly as issues arise.
- Be creative in the delivery of your session. Whenever possible make sure the approach is interactive and two-way, and not just one-way from you to them.

DESIRED SITUATION

You're likely to experience greater engagement and faster results using the coaching method, rather than telling people what to do. As you use the coaching method more, you'll find that your colleagues start coming to you not just with problems, but also possible solutions. They will become more confident in taking over tasks and solving problems independently.

MENTOR JUNIOR STAFF

17

If do are not inclined to do this an an altruistic exercise, then do it selfishly – the best way to get rid of the low value work you do is to teach someone else to want to do it. Mentoring junior staff is the secret to success in this area.

CURRENT & FUTURE ISSUES

Assist junior colleagues to effectively plan their careers and professional development to fulfil their aspirations. Build your positive personal brand as a Master Expert in the meantime. Help junior colleagues navigate your domain speciality, your industry and the organization successfully. Building the foundations of a successful succession plan.

SUGGESTED ACTIVITY

- Consider carefully who might benefit most from your mentorship, bearing in mind their aspirations, aptitude and learning agility. Consider mentoring people outside your direct sphere and invite experts from other divisions to take your colleagues under their wings. Choosing the right person to mentor, and making sure the chemistry is good between you, is a critical success factor.
- Establish the rules of engagement early on, and make sure you are both aware of what is acceptable and isn't in a mentoring situation. You'll find various Mentoring Guides on Expertunity's recommended Learning Portal which provide great advice around how to make these connections successful, and how to avoid serious pitfalls.
- Establish some clear goals of the connection early on. What will you get out of the relationship, and what will they? You'll learn from them as well, and it will also remind you of how it was for you, when you were younger and making your way. This is something worth remembering.
- Make sure they are doing most of the hard work, arranging meetings, suggesting topics, and undertaking the post-session actions they said they would.
- Agree an exit strategy from the beginning. Agree that it is OK for both parties to walk away if it isn't working. Choose an end (let's say six monthly sessions as an initial commitment), so that you can have a good conversation as to whether goals have been achieved, new goals could be set, and exploring whether each party wants to continue.

DESIRED SITUATION

Results from mentoring vary but they usually help you build a reputation for giving back to both your team and the organization. It also helps a more junior colleague progress their skills and knowledge more rapidly than they might have otherwise. Most mentors report learning a great deal from the people they arementoring – what it is like working in other parts of the organization, what it is like as a more junior person in the organization, and the challenges of career development today – rather than when we were in the early stages of our careers. This is very useful intelligence and context that helps our general Knowledge Transfer skills.

18 USE DELEGATION TO HELP DEVELOP MORE JUNIOR STAFF

When junior staff stop learning they leave, and they we are all back to square one – stuck with low level tasks that only we know how to do. Developing junior staff is a "must do", not a "nice to do if I have time".

CURRENT & FUTURE ISSUES

We want junior experts to step up and grow their skills, knowledge and experience. The obvious way for the organization to do this is ensure each expert has a roadmap for professional growth, and that senior experts play their part in coaching and delegating. We want to avoid the situation where junior talent feel stuck and have stopped learning. When this happens, they will seek growth opportunities outside our organization with competitors.

SUGGESTED ACTIVITY

- When choosing who to delegate to, consider the development opportunities for those in your team
- Consider your team members development plans, their aspirational roles, their strengths and challenge areas, and delegate specific tasks as an opportunity to grow their skills and develop your team
- Consider asking a more experienced member in your team to coach/ mentor others on a specific task. By doing this, you are providing an opportunity for your senior team member to practise their coaching skills as well as providing a growth opportunity for your junior team member
- Remember that they may need to "check in" and support some more than others when you have delegated a task. Make sure to let your delegate know to ask you about any questions or concerns and to keep you up-to-date on progress.

DESIRED SITUATION

Valued junior talent will be retained and grown by the business. Senior experts will get time and space to work on higher order tasks and projects.

⑲ DEVELOP DELIBERATE DELEGATION PLANS

Most experts want to build their delegation skills in order to create more time for themselves to work at a higher level of expertise in the organization.

CURRENT & FUTURE ISSUES

Getting stuck doing the same work year after year because you can't find time to work on new interesting higher level work or there is no one available to take over some of your more transactional duties to create this time. Get beyond the single point of failure or dependency – you – in getting core tasks done or problems solved. Helping build their careers also helps you build yours.Create a succession plan and avoid there being none.

SUGGESTED ACTIVITY

- Choose carefully what to delegate. As an expert it is easy for us to want to delegate the unpleasant grunt work. Or we might want to hang on to tasks that we particularly enjoy doing, usually because it is where we generated our reputation for excellence, and it is easy work for us to do.
- Choosing what should be delegated needs to take into account what will interest the person you are delegating to, what is the least risk initially, and what will help both parties develop their career. Delegating only boring grunt work won't work in the long run. Your junior person will get fed up and leave. Be proactive in engaging with those who would benefit from development opportunities through delegation, so they are prepared and happy to take on the tasks when the time comes.
- Choose specific things – perhaps two or three – and work on getting those successfully delegated first.
- Develop a detailed delegation plan, which is staged in considered increments that breaks down the tasks being delegated into manageable chunks and allows both parties to monitor progress. An example of such a plan is available on Expertunity's Learning Portal.
- Consider deploying the Situational Leadership Model (links to the website of the people who developed the model are also on our continuous learning portal) to help you plan and structure the work you delegate.
- Always consider the opportunity to build in incremental innovation into the delegation process, by considering and exploring new ways of achieving things, and not just handing down the way you've always done them.

DESIRED SITUATION

If you choose the right colleague and undertake the right progress you can expect wonderful results – a colleague who is happily growing their skills and knowledge. You also create more time for yourself to work on higher level value creation. If you build in continuous improvement to the delegation process, then you are likely also to see more efficient processes and systems emerge.

03

HOW TO BECOME A MASTER EXPERT

TALENT
DEVELOPER

CAPABILITY: KNOWLEDGE TRANSFER
EXPERT ROLE: TALENT DEVELOPER

MASTER EXPERT

- Owns their own personal growth plan, and makes continuous professional development a priority.
- Oversees junior colleagues' personal growth plans, and provides timely feedback to support execution.
- Creates challenging and stretch opportunities for colleagues; aligned with their career goals.
- Actively identifies and grooms a successor.

EXPERT

- Owns their own personal growth plan, and makes continuous professional development a priority.
- Ensures more junior colleagues have personal growth plans, and provides timely feedback to support execution.

SPECIALIST

- Owns their own personal growth plan, and makes continuous professional development a priority.

DERAILING

- Shows little interest in, and spends no time on helping emerging technical talent develop.
- Considers developing talent a threat to their status and employment.

20 MODEL THE RIGHT BEHAVIOR AND HAVE YOUR OWN PERSONAL GROWTH PLAN

If we aspire to be a Master Expert, we can't behave in one way and expect others to behave differently. Showing the value of having our own Personal Growth Plan, and how we have made it central to our success, is critically important in motivating those associated with us – especially junior experts – to do the same.

CURRENT & FUTURE ISSUES

Create a learning environment where sharing knowledge, experience and skills is part of the culture. Motivate others to learn and to grow. Ensure a lack of currency in skills and knowledge doesn't afflict you or the wider group.

SUGGESTED ACTIVITY

- No one is going to follow your advice about focusing on their development and your message about continuous learning, unless you are modelling the same behavior. Shaping a meaningful and actionable personal growth plan (PGP – see Appendix) is a critical step in setting an example, and the standard, that you will be asking everyone else to follow. Use the Expertship PGP template to identify growth opportunities for you, and some of these may well involve developing skills in others and delegating tasks.
- Once the PGP is in existence, bring it to life by referencing it both personally and across the broader group as something you are consistently working on. It is best that plans are validated by the person you report to (multiple people in the case of many experts), and progress is monitored on a monthly basis. If it is just lodged in the HR system as a compliance gesture then you'll be setting precisely the wrong example to the talent you are hoping to develop.

DESIRED SITUATION

Retain personal currency and relevance. An ability to talk about how you are executing your plan builds personal brand and credibility. In an ideal situation, more junior colleagues will be asking you advice about how to develop their own plans and grow their own skills and knowledge.

21

DEVELOP AN EAGLE EYE FOR UNDER-GROWN TALENT

You and your stakeholders need to know just what information you have available. That way you can ensure it is current and you can work out ways to expand the knowledge base.

CURRENT & FUTURE ISSUES

Ensure there is a pipeline of new experts coming through to serve the organization and provide succession planning opportunities. The junior colleagues who are ambitious and wish to develop are successfully identified and nurtured.

SUGGESTED ACTIVITY

- Develop a description of what it takes to be defined as talent with potential in your technical domain. You may wish to do this with other fellow senior colleagues or get help from the Organizational Development/HR team, whose job is to attract and retain talent with potential.
- It is important the profile of those to be invested in is agreed, to avoid any suspicion of favoritism or luck. Junior colleagues need to earn the right to be heavily invested in. It is important that this description is not just a crude replica of you.
- Make time for 'aspiration discussions' with junior talent as you interact with them on tasks and projects. Ask them what their aspirations are short and long-term, and what they are doing about achieving those goals.
- Some junior staff with the most potential may be either shy, introverted or lacking in confidence, and so won't necessarily envision rapidly developing professional growth. Others who profess to want to grow rapidly may not have the horsepower. You are looking for a combination of aspiration, engagement with the organization and what it does, and capability. If all three boxes are ticked, then they should be on an accelerated professional growth track – and be attending an Expertship program.
- Be aware that many experts find it difficult to articulate what professional growth is, and you may need to help them by sharing the Expertship Model with them.
- Periodically offer opportunities for professional growth via shadowing or places on projects, and watch who puts their hands up. This often is a show of aspiration. If your most talented colleagues are not putting their hands up, ask why.

DESIRED SITUATION

By choosing the right colleagues and undertaking the right progress plans, you can expect wonderful results. You will build a reputation as a 'talent factory' – a department where younger talent is nurtured and developed, and then possibly assigned to higher positions around the organization. Initially this may seem like a negative – you lose your best young talent. But actually, it's a win – because the departments and Master Experts who are known as talent factory attract all the best talent in the first place. Succession planning – particularly your own – becomes easier. It is easier for the organization to give you a new, interesting role or project if they know that you have successfully groomed successors.

(22) DEVELOP A SUCCESSION PLAN

Don't believe for a moment that it is the organization's responsibility to organise a succession plan for you. You're taking a huge risk and anecdotally, it is very unlikely anyone is thinking about how to replace you.

CURRENT & FUTURE ISSUES

If we are a single point of failure, this leaves us stuck in our current role forever. Our leaders can't move us to other roles, or involve us in high value projects, if we are the only person who knows how to undertake particular technical tasks. We need to understand who our successors might be and actively work on positioning them for future success.

SUGGESTED ACTIVITY

- In smaller organizations successors may not exist and therefore we might need to build a case for hiring talent that could succeed (or fill in for us) in the future.
- However, in most medium-sized or large organizations there are plenty of possible successors, if only we could see them. By seeing them, we mean we are open to the possibility they might be our successors. In our experience many experts subconsciously don't believe their unique skills could ever be adequately replaced and so aren't able to identify possible candidates.
- Take an objective view of your own journey – how did you become expert in this field? Often this is a serendipitous journey, and this is useful to know. Consider what very specific capabilities you needed to be successful in your field – beyond technical skills. For example, what learning skills did you need? What motivation was required?
- Ask other experts in your field about their journey to expert mastery – what routes did they take? And ask them about what motivated them to learn as well.
- As a consequence, you'll build a picture of the various talent pools you might be able to mine to find possible successors. You'll also be able to build up a "success profile" – a list of particular attributes that are desirable and an indicator of future success. Note – one day in the past, you had potential but no knowledge ... you are looking for people that looked like you years ago, not people who look like you today.

DESIRED SITUATION

The benefits of identifying successors and beginning to socialize the longterm opportunities for these colleagues are significant for ourselves and for our organizations. Increasingly organizations are waking up to the fact that having single point of failure for technical positions is a critical risk. We are better off being proactive in this space and showing both our capability and motivation to become an effective knowledge sharer and capability builder.

23 BE A TALENT WORTH DEVELOPING

What is our personal learning brand? Do we learn and keep it to ourselves? Do we learn and share? Do we consider being sent to conferences our right, or a privilege? How we show up at and after attending learning events has a huge impact on whether the organization will continue to invest in us.

CURRENT & FUTURE ISSUES

Acknowledging our responsibility to build the capability of others, we don't want to miss out on opportunities to develop. We need to ensure we are seen as worthy of investment.

SUGGESTED ACTIVITY

- Think about what the organization might consider the criteria for "high potential". Your organization almost certainly has a definition of this for people leaders but see if one exists for technical experts.
- Undertake an objective audit of how you may be currently seen by the organization in terms of this definition of potential. At Expertunity, we encourage organizations to consider potential as being the ability to add future value. Are you experienced as a professional who clearly has the capability, aspiration and drive to add more value? Are you seen as ambitious to do so? Has this been clearly communicated? Or not? Are you waiting to be tapped on the shoulder?
- Consider the learning agility signals you are sending. When new projects are floated, do you nominate to be involved, or shirk the extra workload and challenge of learning new things? Are you seen as someone who is already investing in their own learning or are you a passive learner, waiting to be sent on a program or course?
- Do you have a Personal Growth Plan and are you acting upon it independently, or do you have to be policed in order to draft the plan and act upon it?
- Having considered these questions, make a clear plan of action to positively present yourself, authentically, as someone who is ambitious to growth further and add more value, and is, as a consequence, worth investing in.
- Consider also specific programs that you can nominate as being something you aspire to attend.

DESIRED SITUATION

You are seen as someone who has high potential to add significantly more value to the organization if given the chance. You are seen as someone who actively embraces learning opportunities and makes the most of them. When new learning opportunities arise, the organization naturally thinks of you as a possible participant or candidate.

SOLUTIONING

Solves complex technical problems effectively and quickly, via insightful diagnosis, shaping long-term solutions that improve processes and create opportunities.

THE THREE EXPERT ROLES OF SOLUTIONING

PROBLEM IDENTIFIER

Understanding where and why problems occur by deploying objective and complex analysis.

ACTIVE RESPONDER

Responding at an appropriate speed to requests, and getting on the front foot by becoming proactive not reactive, and predicting where requests will come from and why.

PROBLEM SOLVER

Seeing problems through to resolution, and working towards delivering long term solutions.

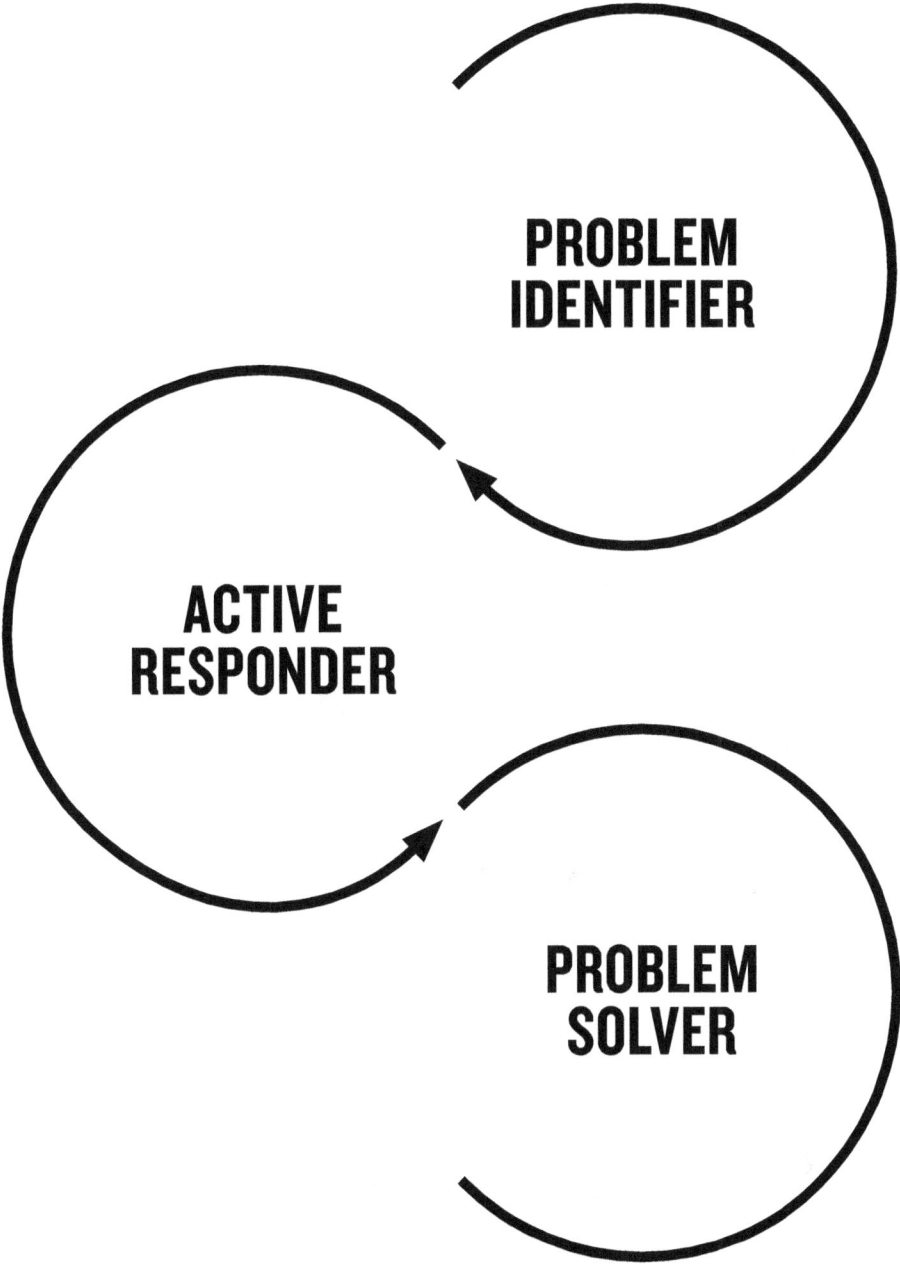

PROBLEM IDENTIFIER

ACTIVE RESPONDER

PROBLEM SOLVER

01

HOW TO BECOME A MASTER EXPERT

PROBLEM IDENTIFIER

CAPABILITY: SOLUTIONING
EXPERT ROLE: PROBLEM IDENTIFIER

MASTER EXPERT	• Promotes new ways of looking at current problems. • Highly skilled at identifying all problems, regardless of complexity. • Addresses symptoms and accurately identifies all likely underlying causes and likely implications.
EXPERT	• Accurately identifies common and uncommon problems. • Analyses complex problems effectively. • Addresses symptoms and accurately identifies likely underlying causes.
SPECIALIST	• Accurately identifies common problems. • Developing the ability to analyse complex problems. • Unlikely to consider underlying causes.
DERAILING	• Struggles to identify common problems with consistent accuracy. • Cannot analyse complex problems, or consider underlying causes. • Conducts problem identification from a narrow, wholly technical viewpoint.

(24) ADOPT A CONSULTING APPROACH

When engaged to address a problem, undertake a detailed discovery of the related issues. This should include gathering relevant evidence of how those issues show up and the impact they have on the organization and its KPIs.

CURRENT & FUTURE ISSUES

If we merely 'take the order' we are adding no value. We remain ignorant of the underlying business intent. And, worst case scenario, the solution that the requesting stakeholder has asked us to implement may prove ineffective. If we fail to consult about the underlying issues, evidence and impact, and we merely implement others' proposed solutions, we are at least partly responsible for any ensuing problems or missed opportunities.

SUGGESTED ACTIVITY

• While assuring the stakeholder who has requested your input that you are keen to assist them, ask the following series of questions:

- What are some of the issues you or the organization have been facing due to the problem presented?
- Which of those issues are most crucial to resolve?
- How are those crucial issues showing up? Ideally you will uncover some quantifiable data about one or more organizational measures that matter.
- What are the impacts on the organization of those issues remaining unresolved? Based on the quantitative data, there may be a way of calculating the monetary value of closing the gap between current and desired performance.

DESIRED SITUATION

Asking these questions and gathering the relevant data will provide you and the stakeholder with greater insight as to what problem you are actually trying to solve. It will provide a holistic understanding of everything that needs to be in place for the underlying organizational issues to be addressed – not merely the technical input. You can bring more of your expertise to bear and ensure that your solutions are holistically designed. This means they are more likely to have the intended organizational impact. This approach will positively enhance your brand. You will be perceived as more strategic and more outcomes-focused.

25 COMMIT TO SUSPEND JUDGEMENT, AND LISTEN INSTEAD

It isn't possible to reach Master Expert level by thinking we already know it all. In fact, the definition of Master Expert is a non-stop curiosity to discover what we don't know but could or should. For some of us, this means a complete shift in the way we listen to others.

CURRENT & FUTURE ISSUES

As busy experts we have a tendency to jump to quick conclusions about what the problem is, and then swiftly propose a solution. We wish to avoid assuming we know what the problem is before proper discovery questions. We also wish to avoid being dismissive and appearing uncaring by declaring we know the answer very quickly in front of stakeholders, which may appear arrogant.

SUGGESTED ACTIVITY

- You will commit to listening carefully to everything your clients and colleagues are telling you, interrogate them to check carefully you've completely understood the issue, before moving to solution.
- Even though it sounds like the same issue you've heard many times before, you will avoid jumping to the same conclusion until your clarifying questions have made you certain it is the right solution.
- As a discipline, you will consider what else the problem could be before deciding on your first view to ensure you are not missing something.

DESIRED SITUATION

As busy as we are, by taking a little extra time we'll be sure we are right by proper due diligence, and we'll build a positive brand by taking extra time to make sure we are hearing our stakeholders and colleagues effectively.

26 CONDUCT A PATTERN ANALYSIS

Doing the same thing and expecting a different result is the definition of insanity. If you are explaining to people how to do something for the twentieth time that week, you're the problem. It's time to consider why something is happening rather than just responding as before.

CURRENT & FUTURE ISSUES

Stop spending a disproportionate amount of time fixing the same old issues whilst higher value – and less routine – activities end up receiving insufficient attention.

SUGGESTED ACTIVITY

- Make a list of the most common problems that you're asked to address or requests that are raised.
- Analyze whether or not there are any patterns to the sorts of needs people have, or the or issues they face. Is there a disproportionate number of the same kind of request – or issues stemming from the same process, or piece of software, etc? Does the disproportionate number of problems arising indicate some kind of common cause – e.g. that there's a need to re-engineer the process, or is there perhaps a need for a training program that might, for a finite investment of time, get many of the requests to go away?
- Keep a log over a few weeks of every issue or problem or request raised. Analyze whether there are any over-represented types of issues or common root causes. If so, there is an opportunity to develop some proactive ways of preventing such issues from arising. At least, if the problems are truly unavoidable, this will ensure that you're adequately resourced and able to address them swiftly.

DESIRED SITUATION

This will allow you to free up your time for the more strategic value-added activities than the routine same old set of stuff. It will also potentially spare your stakeholders unnecessary hassles.

27 CREATE AND MANAGE A RISK REGISTER

This is a common project management activity. It is a way of anticipating and preparing for future problems.

CURRENT & FUTURE ISSUES

Being caught off guard by risks that could have been anticipated and prevented, or at least planned for and offset.

Looking incompetent because the organisation was expecting you to anticipate risk events. Being in danger of severe reprimand because someone will need to be blamed, and you are in the firing line. Wanting to be seen as someone who can contribute at a higher level because you have the ability to see into the future and warn the organisation of future risks before they occur.

SUGGESTED ACTIVITY

- Not all risks are created equal. Apart from feeling yourself to be on the front foot by identifying upfront all potential risks, mitigating strategies for those risks which appear to carry the most severe impacts can be prioritised.
- Use a table or spreadsheet such as the one below in which you (and, ideally your stakeholders) can explore all potential risks. A risk is a potential future problem that may or may not arise. By identifying them prior to their manifesting, you have a chance to prevent them or at least minimize their negative impacts.

RISK	Potential Severity of Impact (H-M-L)	Likelihood of Occurring (H-M-L)	How the risk might be mitigated, prevented, etc.

DESIRED SITUATION

Undertaking a simple risk analysis and planning for possible snags will enable you to significantly shrink the subsequent number of problems arising. At the very least, it will reduce the disruption caused by unanticipated issues.

(28) LOOK BEYOND TO ANTICIPATE FUTURE PROBLEMS

If we aspire to operate at Master Expert level we have to be future-focussed. This means seeing around corners. To what extent do we have smart systems, and time allocated, to allow us to do this effectively?

CURRENT & FUTURE ISSUES

In our journey to Master Expert when it comes to solutioning we are seeking to anticipate and prepare for future problems we will need to identify. By definition these are problems that we have yet to experience – and perhaps our organizations have yet to experience. Our ability to detect early warning signals for new problems enables us to be far more effective in dealing with them.

SUGGESTED ACTIVITY

- On the principle that it's very likely someone in the world is or has already experienced new problems in our field, we need to consider what mechanisms are available to us to find out who these people are, where they are, and how they initially identified, and then eventually fixed the problem. Is it conferences, webinars, publications or leveraging social networks?
- Are there forums which we can join that discuss and predict future problems?
- Are there people on your network that can be leveraged – "any new problems arising in your part of the world, or industry?" This assumes your network is external and broad (see stakeholder engagement for suggestions on network building).

DESIRED SITUATION

- We have developed an early warning system that keeps us up-to-date on future problems that may develop, and the prevention strategies others are adopting to either mitigate the likelihood the problem will occur, or the new solutions they are deploying to solve new problems.

02

HOW TO BECOME A MASTER EXPERT

ACTIVE
RESPONDER

CAPABILITY: SOLUTIONING
EXPERT ROLE: ACTIVE RESPONDER

MASTER EXPERT	• Active responder, advanced prioritization skills. • Facilitator of responses from others, leveraging network. • Proactively uncovers or predicts emergent requirements to facilitate real-time responses to market changes. • Initiates contact in anticipation of emerging requirements.
EXPERT	• Responds to problems as proactively as possible, seeking longer term solutions as well as immediate fixes. • Responds with appropriate speed congruent with the criticality of the problem. • Routinely updates needs analysis to address changing requirements.
SPECIALIST	• Responds to problems reactively, but in a timely fashion. • Tends to respond sequentially to problems as reported, rather than prioritizing.
DERAILING	• Responds to problems reactively, selectively and in either a reluctant or slow manner. • Unresponsive.

(29) LEARN OF STAKEHOLDERS' PLANS AND EMERGING REQUIREMENTS

If your stakeholders are telling us only what they think we need to know then we have the wrong relationship with them, and the bad news is that it is our fault. We need to know everything, because stakeholders often don't really know what we need to know.

CURRENT & FUTURE ISSUES

Avoid last minute surprises – where you're not adequately resourced or prepared to address new requirements, or over-invested to address requirements that are no longer valid.
Develop the ability to avoid rework, streamline delivery, and anticipate requirements

SUGGESTED ACTIVITY

- Routinely schedule proactive discovery conversations with key stakeholders to learn of their emerging challenges and initiatives. Anticipate requirements and make timely provisions for them.
- Book a meeting with each key stakeholder – particularly those that depend on you to deliver for them. Explain that you're keen to ensure the timely and efficient delivery of their requirements. You're keen to learn of their plans and the possible implications these might have on their future requirements.
- You'll need to be sensitive to the possibility that some stakeholders may not have given detailed consideration to their plans. In these cases, you may want to stress that you're not seeking to lock down an exact prediction of future requirements. You just want to get a general indication of their direction.
- Ask some pertinent questions. Will their requirements stay mostly the same? Do they have any new strategies planned? Are there any market changes that might dictate a revised approach and new requirements?
- Once you have built up a picture of likely future requirements, you can take the steps to focus on the most significant requirements. This might include readying processes and systems, upskilling, planning resources, etc., so that you can respond efficiently and effectively in real time when the requirements surface.

DESIRED SITUATION

Readiness and an immediacy of response. Anticipating stakeholders' needs before the demand is urgent. An ability to align and budget resources to requirements ahead of time.

(30) AUDIT HOW YOUR CUSTOMERS EXPERIENCE YOU

How difficult are we to deal with? Do we know? Do we care?
We'd better – there is a reason expert departments get outsourced,
and it's because they have failed to engage properly with
stakeholders and get regular feedback.

CURRENT & FUTURE ISSUES

Sometimes stakeholders' experiences of seeking to engage experts are not what we would wish. This can lead to a souring of relationships or make them less likely to approach you or other experts in the future.

SUGGESTED ACTIVITY

- Analyze how easy it is for your stakeholders to engage with you. Do you have any default responses which they might take issue with? Are you unresponsive or do you appear hassled or annoyed? How would you like those 'moments of truth' to play out in an ideal world?
- It may be helpful to survey them about how they view your responsiveness. Are they generally satisfied with what you do? If not, is there a pattern to what they're dissatisfied with?
- Where necessary, remove any problematic hurdles. Some of the shortfalls in the stakeholder experience might be process-related. Perhaps the steps in the process weren't designed with the human experience in mind, and are technical procedures.
- At other times, the shortfalls may be entirely behavioral. Either way, both types of issues can be addressed through intentional redesign.
- Design and engineer the ideal stakeholder experience – their journey from first contact through to total satisfaction. This is a common practice in customer experience initiatives. Create a flowchart starting with the point of first contact through to the confirmation of a successful resolution.
- Determine precisely how you would like each step of the process to be experienced by the stakeholder. For example, when they raise a ticket:
  - What type of response would you prefer they experience for them to think positively (and realistically) about you and your team?
  - How should they be kept informed while you are working on their problem?
  - How would you like them to experience the closing out of the issue?
  - Once you have mapped the ideal stakeholder journey, ensure you are able to deliver it consistently.

DESIRED SITUATION

By applying some design to stakeholders' experiences when they approach you, you will set up an environment for happier stakeholders who will regard you as helpful and responsive. You'll have paced their expectations about such things as your preferred lead times and data requirements, and your preferred focus and priorities. They're more likely to engage you constructively – in the right way and at the right time.

㉛ IDENTIFY FUTURE DIRECTIONS, REQUIREMENTS AND POTENTIAL PROBLEMS

The ability to understand what our stakeholders will ask (or demand?) from us in three years' time is what turns and Expert into a Master Expert. This ability stops us building services for our stakeholders that will be shortly obsolete.

CURRENT & FUTURE ISSUES

Without taking the time to identify, anticipate and prepare for emerging requirements, opportunities and problems, we can often find ourselves having to respond in crisis mode once those issues or opportunities are already upon us but we will have insufficient capacity or time to respond effectively.

SUGGESTED ACTIVITY

- Apply the SCAN-FOCUS-ACT methodology (see Appendix ii) to identify emerging issues and opportunities. Brainstorm anticipated future requirements and plan for timely provision. This is another approach to uncovering or predicting potential requirements. It's a piece of analysis that you can conduct individually, although it's typically more fruitful if you involve a diverse set of stakeholders.
- If you can get everyone interacting and building off each other's ideas, then this approach will elicit more ideas and insights. If this is not possible, then you can either interview or survey them separately with a common set of future-focused questions.
  - Scan focuses on exploring all the possible future scenarios – strategic choices your organization is contemplating, moves from competitors or other players in its industry, the evolution of various meta-trends (political, environmental, sociological, technical), etc.
  - Focus zeroes in on the potential issues or opportunities that you consider most likely and highest impact – prioritizing from all the possible actions you could take as a consequence of the scan.
  - Act is determining precisely what proactive initiatives you undertake either to immunize your organization from emerging problems or to capitalize on opportunities – and, of course, taking timely action.

DESIRED SITUATION

While it's impossible to fully predict the future, conducting this analysis should result in fewer surprises than being ill prepared. Often you will be able to identify, anticipate and prepare for emergent challenges and opportunities. If you engage key stakeholders in the process, then you can collectively develop a shared understanding and readiness.

32

DESIGN A RESPONSE REGIME THAT RESPECTFULLY MANAGES STAKEHOLDER EXPECTATIONS

Managing stakeholder expectations – as opposed to simply complaining about their unreasonableness – is something every success expert has to master. It means developing the ability to diplomatically and artfully say no.

CURRENT & FUTURE ISSUES

When inundated with requests, even the best experts tend to favour some tasks and are unresponsive to others. We wish to avoid the consequences of a "no reply" situation, that negatively impacts our professional brand and leaves us open to criticism from some stakeholders.

SUGGESTED ACTIVITY

- As an expert, you will receive more requests for assistance than you can reasonably handle and will be unable to respond to some requests. Consider which requests are the least important and urgent to respond to and start to build a "response regime" for those requests.
- Response regimes help you manage stakeholders' expectations in a respectful manner.
- You might deploy a prepared email (that you cut and paste) which explains the project pressure you are under which is interfering with your ability to respond in a timely fashion to assistance requests (perhaps with some alternatives for action that the stakeholder might take). Here you are predicting the sorts of requests that you won't be able to deal with, and providing links perhaps to manuals or other resources that might be able to help them; you are actively responding, in a timely fashion, but saying you can't help.
- You might deploy (for more important stakeholders) a phone call, perhaps leaving a voicemail, acknowledging the request but personally telling the stakeholder that due to circumstances beyond your control, as important as it is to them, you're not available to help them; "please call back and I'll explain". If they call back (and many will not), you'll be ready to explain how multiple projects have stacked up and you've been instructed to get them finished and exclude work on all other requests. You maintain the relationship, actively respond, and indicate their importance by this process, but still don't execute the work.
- You may have multiple other options available to you, but the purpose of this initiative is to prepare responses ahead of their arrival, so you can respond actively and in a timely fashion but still minimise disruption time, and possible damage to the relationship.

DESIRED SITUATION

Requests that can't be dealt with are managed respectfully, with honesty and in a timely fashion. Stakeholders will understand early that their needs will not be immediately addressed.

03

HOW TO BECOME A MASTER EXPERT

PROBLEM SOLVER

CAPABILITY: SOLUTIONING
EXPERT ROLE: PROBLEM SOLVER

MASTER EXPERT

- Expert in all common and uncommon problems.
- Shapes long term solutions from a technical, business, and systemic perspective.
- Promotes new ways of looking at current solutions, and challenges current practices.
- Proactively puts in place strategies to future-proof against known problems.
- Sees solution through to realising benefits.

EXPERT

- Collects experience of common and uncommon scenarios.
- Provides accurate solutions to common and uncommon problems.
- Seeks to future proof regularly occurring problems.
- Approaches solutioning by considering both technical and business perspectives.

SPECIALIST

- Collecting experiences of common scenarios.
- Provides accurate solutions to common problems.
- Approaches solutioning from a mostly technical perspective.

DERAILING

- Relies on past experience to solve problems.
- Conducts problem solutioning from a narrow, wholly technical viewpoint.
- Jumps to solutioning prior to properly understanding all requirements & context.
- Overly rigid and uncompromising application of methodologies.

33

DEPLOY 'OUTSIDE-IN' THINKING

Everyone is talking about the need to be more customer centric. This doesn't just mean thinking about customers more (Expert level); it means putting ourselves in the customer's shoes (Master Expert level).

CURRENT & FUTURE ISSUES

Coming at problems from the same angle all the time will mean that some solutions might be invisible to you. This reduces your problem-solving effectiveness, and leaves you open to be superseded by someone with a fresh perspective.

SUGGESTED ACTIVITY

- Solving problems from the 'inside-out' means we deploy our current understanding of all of the issues. When we start thinking 'outside-in', we put ourselves in the position of the customer, and see the problem that they want solving from their perspective. This change of perspective often means we see solutions that might not otherwise be viable to us.
- Future 'outside-in' thinking is where you imagine the value being delivered to the customer in three years' time, perhaps by a competitor unencumbered by the legacy systems and responsibilities of your current organization. This enables you to have a clear picture of where you need to get to, and perhaps means you decide you have to change your approach entirely. While an incremental fix might work this time, it won't solve the long-term value need of the customer.

DESIRED SITUATION

Ability to see long-term issues and solutions rather than just operating on a short-term fix basis. Ability to think more holistically about customer value. Ability to envisage the future, a strong personal brand value trait.

34 CONDUCT AND REPORT IMPACT ANALYSIS

If we want our organisation to understand the value we add as experts, then we need to give them some help in doing so. That is, assuming of course, we know how to measure the value we add.

CURRENT & FUTURE ISSUES

All too often, even when our solutions have added value, that value is hidden. An impact analysis gives us the opportunity to demonstrate our value and improve the quality of our solutions by carefully gathering and citing evidence.

SUGGESTED ACTIVITY

- When someone brings us an issue to be addressed, we can ask evidence questions such as: "how (or where) precisely is the issue showing up?" If this doesn't give us an answer then we can follow up with an impact question such as "then what happens?" The goal is to identify a KPI that we're being asked to assist the organization in improving.
- Stakeholder's concern: "The system is too slow." Our response: "How can we measure that it has speeded up as a consequence of any solutions we might apply?" And, more importantly: "What is the payoff if we can improve its speed – or the payout if we can't?"
- By measuring the relevant KPI prior to the implementation of our solution – and then again afterwards – we can compare how far the needle has moved. By comparing the shift to the same measures for a control group, we can assert with reasonable confidence that any difference between the two groups is because of our solution.
- Using this approach, we become more focused on ensuring that we have made an impact, rather than simply providing the requester what they asked for. When we become committed to ensuring that the needle moves then our solutions naturally become more holistic, and not merely technical.

DESIRED SITUATION

When we have sound evidence that our solutions have had a positive, measurable impact then we can report progress and show that benefits have been realized. These reports are best documented in a brief and stakeholder-friendly document or PowerPoint slideshow but will likely get even more attention if also presented in person. Our stakeholders will see us as commercially-oriented, results-or outcomes-focused, delivering high impact and merely by adopting such an approach, we heighten the likelihood of delivering impactful solutions since we know what outcomes we're aiming them at.

35 SHIFT INTO ACTIVE PREVENTION MODE

Fire-fighting, or fire prevention? Where do we currently spend our time, and how do we spend more time on the latter? And if we have time to spend on prevention, what activities should we undertake?

CURRENT & FUTURE ISSUES

If we fail to engage in sufficient prevention, then we'll end up locked into a reactive cycle – perpetually mending things after the fact. It can be heroic to be the person or the team who rescues a project or the organization from imminent disaster but it can also be exhausting.

In addition, tackling problems once they have already begun to impact the organization or its stakeholders is not as effective as identifying them ahead of time and preventing them. Someone still suffers the ill effects of the issue until it gets resolved.

SUGGESTED ACTIVITY

- Next time you resolve a problem, particularly if it is a significant one, conduct a review. You may be able to carry out a review individually, but there can often be advantages in engaging others in the review – more ideas, shared understanding and commitment. This will help shape your brand as someone who cares about and is committed to prevention.
- What is the likelihood of the problem recurring? If it's likely, and the impact is significant, then identify how exactly the problem arose and how it might be prevented from happening again. Or, if it's not possible to prevent it, how you can most expediently mobilize an effective response to it and minimize adverse effects. Plan to put these preventative or swift responses in place before the problem arises again – and ensure that you execute.

DESIRED SITUATION

Through regular reviews and developing preventative action plans, you will develop a reputation for being strategic. You will spend less time fighting fires.

(36) BRING CREATIVITY TO THE TABLE

In order to bring new thinking to the table we need to somehow find the time to do some thinking. And we shouldn't make the mistake of thinking this is best achieved as a solo activity.

CURRENT & FUTURE ISSUES

If we do not make time and space to allow ourselves to be creative, our inspiration to come up with new ideas will be limited. This may mean the quality of solutions we recommend and implement for our customers and organization will have less of an impact on things like operational efficiency, growth strategy or competitive advantage.

SUGGESTED ACTIVITY

- Be proactive and create specific times in your week with the intention to think creatively and move away from the day-to-day operations. Make a meeting with yourself in your diary.
- Draw on your deep, long-term inspiration. Focus on the big impact that you want to have in your role that really matters. Have this big picture impact in mind when you take time to think hard and leverage your creativity.
- Carefully select the space where you do your thinking. Typically, experts find a quiet space where we are able to reduce the "noise" of day-to-day activities. Interruptions destroy the ability to focus on thinking. This might be a physical activity, like a walk.
- Document thoughts and ideas in a single place – no one solves a problem in one session. Use this documentation to re-start subsequent thinking sessions, and indeed re-evaluate previous thoughts? Do you have new information, new insights? Can you remember why you thought that? Creativity is a process, not a light bulb event (the light bulb moment is as a consequence of the process).
- Adopt a curious mindset. Question and consider all options available to you when considering a solution or approach. If you are sure you are right about something, take the alternative view – assume you are wrong and build a case as to why you might be.
- Cultivate creative thinking among colleagues and teams and stakeholders you work with. Create space for creative discussion in project meetings. Take the lead on setting the frame around being curious and creative. Some questions you could ask are:

- What if ... we did it this way instead?   - Imagine if...
- "If" we were to do that....   - Let's explore that more...
  "how" would we begin?   how could that work?

DESIRED SITUATION

Ability to find space and create inspired solutions that are future-focused and beneficial for your team, customer and organization.
Contributes to the organization's values, culture and brand as being innovative, creative and solutions-focused.

PART 2

THE
VALUE
DOMAIN

MARKET CONTEXT

Acquires, retains, refreshes and deploys contextual organizational, competitive and customer knowledge effectively.

THE THREE EXPERT ROLES OF MARKET CONTEXT

ORGANIZATIONAL NAVIGATION

Understanding and traversing the entire organization, and making contributions at departmental, whole-of-organization and where relevant, global levels.

COMPETITIVE ANALYST

Understanding the competitive landscape from a wide-ranging external business and community perspective.

CUSTOMER STRATEGIST

Deploying customer-centric thinking and action, applied to both internal and external customers, and those who are current, prospective, and future customers.

01
ORGANIZATIONAL
NAVIGATOR

02
COMPETITIVE
ANALYST

03
CUSTOMER
STRATEGIST

01

HOW TO BECOME A MASTER EXPERT

ORGANIZATIONAL NAVIGATOR

CAPABILITY: MARKET CONTEXT
EXPERT ROLE: ORGANIZATIONAL NAVIGATOR

MASTER EXPERT	• Advanced understanding and comprehensive knowledge of the global organization. • Understands, is able to articulate, and demonstrates a commitment to global and local strategy. • Navigates complex political landscapes within the organization to achieve goals.
EXPERT	• Comprehensive understanding and knowledge of the immediate organization. • Understands and clearly communicates current local strategy. • Interacts with other departments and functions with clear understanding of their objectives.
SPECIALIST	• Knowledge of how their department contributes to the immediate organization. • Understands departmental plan. • Knowledge of how the organization operates is limited to immediate environment.
DERAILING	• Siloed view of role and department. • Focuses on task and short-term outcomes rather than long-term goals of the department or organization.

GET INFORMED ABOUT AND ALIGN WITH THE ORGANIZATION'S STRATEGY

37

It isn't possible to be strategic without understanding our own organization's strategy, and how this compares and contrasts with our competitors. It isn't about just reading the slide deck – it is obtaining and being able to articulate a much deeper understanding of the strategies the organization rejected to get to this strategy.

CURRENT & FUTURE ISSUES

You need to be aware of, and be a promoter of, your organization's strategy. If you are not, you will be seen as a necessary evil. Worse, you will be regarded as a burdensome cost or distraction from the main game. This reduces the value and relevance of whatever you're putting forward and engaged with.

SUGGESTED ACTIVITY

- Build a connection or alliance with the organization's strategy team. If you work for a small organization, then you can most likely directly approach a senior manager. If you work for a larger organization then there are often more junior members of a larger strategy team that can be approachable and helpful or, your manager might also be willing to assist and be suitably informed. Explain that your intention is to better understand the market context of the organization so that you can more effectively align your expertise, solutions and services with the organization's strategic imperatives.
- Familiarize yourself with the organization's underlying analysis of the market. This will likely mean getting your hands on customer data, competitor analysis and other data sources that inform the organization's strategy. The strategy team will have typically gathered all kinds of data to help inform their thinking. They are often willing to share this data. At the very least, get the strategy document itself and ask one of its authors to talk you through it and the rationale behind it.
- Practise articulating the strategy, its underlying rationale and the line of sight between it and what you, as an expert, do. As an expert in a support function, how easy is it for you and others to make a connection between your daily activities and the organization's highest priorities?
- You need to be fully informed about the strategy in the context of the market, to align your activities with strategic imperatives and to demonstrate that you are committed to total organizational success – not just your technical craft.

DESIRED SITUATION

You will be able to reference the strategy while demonstrating a grasp of its underlying principles. You will be able to show the linkages with your program of work, which will elevate your brand beyond technical contributor to trusted adviser. Your proposals will carry more weight. You'll be consulted more deeply and earlier in the thought process. Your work will be considered essential to organizational success.

38 # MAKE EXPLICIT REFERENCE TO THE ORGANIZATIONAL STRATEGY

The art of influence is to be able to link everything we do – and ask for – to organisational strategy and purpose.

CURRENT & FUTURE ISSUES

Ensure people see the critical relevance or value of the work you do, by making explicit linkages to the organizational strategy.

SUGGESTED ACTIVITY

- Practise translating the strategy in terms that other experts and stakeholders will appreciate and relate to. Clearly identify their contribution to it. Describe the implications of the strategy for whichever group of people you happen to be addressing, and show them how they can best contribute to it. The idea is to illustrate precisely how your particular activities essentially support the organization reaching its goals.
- Align your priorities to be consistent with the strategy. If an activity isn't essential to the strategy– or is even contrary to it– then its validity is questionable. Make explicit linkages in any reports or recommendations you write. The intention is to be both clearly aligned with and connected to the strategy – as well as being seen to be so.

DESIRED SITUATION

Being able to reference the strategy – while demonstrating a grasp of its underlying principles – elevates your brand beyond technical contributor to trusted adviser. If you show the linkages with your program of work your proposals will carry more weight. You'll be consulted more deeply and earlier in the thought process. Your work will be considered essential to organizational success.

39 BECOME A STUDENT OF ORGANIZATIONAL DECISION-MAKING

In order to navigate the organization effectively, we need to understand the how and why of organizational decision-making.

CURRENT & FUTURE ISSUES

Making proposals that are doomed to failure because of the way they are framed, documented, or poorly socialised across stakeholders is a waste of our time, and adds to the frustration we may feel about not being understood. Conversely, having a clear understanding of the complex decision-making process that leads to proposals being accepted, funded and executed gives us a feeling of achievement, and is evidence of how we can add value.

SUGGESTED ACTIVITY

- Every organization makes decisions differently, and typically, there are some key players who are involved in almost every major decision, and they will have ways of working, ways of thinking, and pet hates or mantras that they use to green or red-light proposals and projects. In order to be best able to frame proposals and recommendations effectively, you should aim to understand who these decision-makers are, how they operate and why they operate that way.
- Seek out those who work most closely with these decision-makers and ask about their style and decision-making settings.
- Explore major decisions that the organization has made recently – how did these decisions get made, what process did those recommending the initiative use? How long did it take?
- Dump the "they don't listen to me" mindset and get proactive about understanding who these decision-makers do listen to and why.
- Work closely with existing stakeholders and develop a set of questions designed to help you understand how the political structure of the organization works. "Who would need to be convinced by my recommendation for it to get approval? What particular components of my recommendation would appeal to them and why? Which elements would be unappealing and why? What type of approach do they respond well to, and which do they not?

DESIRED SITUATION

Politically savvy colleagues don't have better recommendations than you do, they may just present them more effectively. With research and consideration, we can expect our recommendations to get more air time, and eventually be accepted if we understand and adapt to the way in which our organizations make recommendations. We'll move from frustration to excitement that our valuable suggestions are being taken seriously and acted upon.

02

HOW TO BECOME A MASTER EXPERT

COMPETITIVE ANALYST

CAPABILITY: MARKET CONTEXT
EXPERT ROLE: COMPETITIVE ANALYST

MASTER EXPERT	<ul><li>Advanced knowledge of the competitive environment in which the organization operates.</li><li>Assesses relative strengths and weaknesses of the organization versus competitors.</li><li>Considers the genesis of future competitors.</li><li>Regular interaction with external customers.</li></ul>
EXPERT	<ul><li>Developing knowledge of the competitive environment in which the organization operates.</li><li>Good knowledge of own organization's competitive position.</li><li>Some exposure to external customers.</li></ul>
SPECIALIST	<ul><li>Limited knowledge of the competitive environment in which the organization operates.</li><li>Limited exposure—if any—to external customers.</li></ul>
DERAILING	<ul><li>Siloed approach to the role, with limited knowledge, or interest, in external factors.</li><li>Limited knowledge of organizational competitors.</li><li>Internal focus.</li></ul>

(40) CONDUCT A COMPETITOR ANALYSIS

The rest of the business tends to sit up and take notice when we offer to provide extra competitive advantage. The only way to do this is to understand the competitors.

CURRENT & FUTURE ISSUES

You should aim to be seen as an authority on the competitive landscape. In the absence of having a clear sense of the organization's competitors, the landscape in which they're competing and their respective strategies, you will be viewed as internally-focussed, unconcerned with and largely irrelevant to the organization's main game.

SUGGESTED ACTIVITY

- Build a relationship with the strategy team (see Organizational Navigator above). Build an understanding of the alternative strategies at play within your organization's competitors. Identify the strategies through which your organization's competitors are hoping to win more business.
- Identify the competing value propositions that each of your competitors – and your own organization – are offering. A value proposition is a concept of which clear, measurable and demonstrable benefits consumers get when buying a particular product or service. What specifically is it that convinces purchasers and consumers that a particular product or service is better than others on the market? Value propositions serve as the basis for competitive advantage when consumers pick that particular product or service over other competitors because they perceive greater value.

DESIRED SITUATION

Clarity about the competitive landscape will allow you to develop solutions – and sell them to stakeholders – that increase your organization's competitive advantage.

41 CONDUCT A SWOT ANALYSIS

Our ability as experts to be objective when completing a SWOT analysis is what gives us the ability to add real insight and value to the rest of the business. Conducting a SWOT analysis isn't an event – it's a continuing process.

CURRENT & FUTURE ISSUES

You need to gain a clear understanding of the relative strengths and weaknesses of your organization in comparison to its competitors, and the opportunities and threats that apply. Without this it will be hard to identify what the highest priority needs of the organization are for the best application of your expertise.

SUGGESTED ACTIVITY

- Undertake a SWOT analysis comparing your organization with its competitors:
  - What are each organization's respective Strengths? What are the positive attributes that provide it with a potential competitive advantage? It's not merely a positive attribute but a positive attribute that affords it an advantage because it is something that competitors don't have – at least not to the same degree.
  - What are each organization's respective Weaknesses? What are its vulnerabilities, shortfalls or handicaps which do not apply to competitors and result in a competitive disadvantage?
  - What are each organization's respective Opportunities? What are potential moves the organization could make to increase its competitive advantage? Unlike Strengths and Weaknesses, these can be common to all organizations being compared.
  - What are each organization's respective Threats? What are the potential exposures to the organization that could adversely impact its competitive performance? As with Opportunities, Threats can be common across all organizations in your comparison.
- The goal of a SWOT analysis is to identify ways in which you can create a new strength to increase your organization's competitive advantage – a positive attribute that your competitors don't have – or further strengthen an existing strength making it immune to competitive threats. For it to offer meaningful competitive advantage, it should be a strength that matters to customers.
- Take advantage of one or more opportunities. This will help insulate the organization against risks.
- Eliminate or at least reduce a weakness – or better exploit competitors' weaknesses.

DESIRED SITUATION

Increased competitive advantage for your organization. A SWOT analysis can be conducted as a solo activity but there are significant benefits in conducting it alongside stakeholders. This will give you shared understanding and insight, and collective ownership of any ensuing strategies.

42

CONDUCT A PORTER'S FIVE FORCES ANALYSIS

Some models are no use at all, and some are crucial to understand, and Porter's Five Forces model, if you want to be taken seriously as strategic and commercial by the business – is close to top of the list. Just by having the conversations and undertaking the research to be able to populate it will change the way we think about our organisation, its challenges, and the value we could add.

CURRENT & FUTURE ISSUES

Porter's Five Forces Analysis provides significant insight into the various strategic influences at play inside the industry or market context that your organization operates in. If you don't have these insights, it is hard to align and position your solutions to have critical impact on the organization's performance.

SUGGESTED ACTIVITY

- This analysis goes beyond competitor analysis and examines other forces at work in the industry that influence an organization's ability to make a profit. While the framework in the Appendix iii raises other aspects to consider, we recommend that you at least explore the following:
  - *Competitive Rivalry* – Is the market still growing or are competitors in the industry fiercely competing over market share? Is there an oversupply of competitors? How much opportunity for differentiation is there – or is it all about price? How cheap or easy is it for customers to switch between suppliers?
  - *Supplier Power* – How dependent are you and your competitors on a limited number of suppliers (In which case those suppliers can charge a higher price)? How significant are these costs in relation to what you and your competitors charge? Could those suppliers potentially bypass you and go direct to market? How significant are switching costs?
  - *Buyer Power* – How much choice do buyers have? Could those buyers potentially bypass you and go straight to suppliers? Which purchasing criteria matter most to buyers?
  - *New Entrant Power* – What would it take for a new competitor to enter part or all of the market?
  - *Substitute Power* – How else might buyers address their needs without using either you or your competitors' products and services?

DESIRED SITUATION

As with all development suggestions in the Market Context area, there is an inherent conceptual payoff in terms of fluency of understanding. However, such a conceptual grasp of market context will typically prompt you to take action to help your organization compete more effectively in the markets it plays in. Porter's Five Forces analysis can also be informative for expert functions – which might think themselves immune to competitive forces. Where there are so many disruptive forces in the world – including outsourcing of shared service functions as well as technologically-mediated substitutes – unless the experts are clearly adding value then they might be viewed as costs to be cut.

03

HOW TO BECOME A MASTER EXPERT

CUSTOMER STRATEGIST

CAPABAILITY: MARKET CONTEXT
EXPERT ROLE: COMPETITIVE ANALYST

MASTER EXPERT	• Advanced knowledge of the competitive environment in which the organization operates. • Assess relative strengths and weaknesses of the organization versus competitors. • Considers the genesis of future competitors. • Regular interaction with external customers.
EXPERT	• Developing knowledge of the competitive environment in which the organization operates. • Good knowledge of own organization's competitive position. • Some exposure to external customers.
SPECIALIST	• Limited knowledge of the competitive environment in which the organization operates. • Limited exposure—if any—to external customers.
DERAILING	• Siloed approach to the role, with limited knowledge, or interest, in external factors. • Limited knowledge of organizational competitors. • Internal focus.

(43) GET YOURSELF ACROSS THE ORGANIZATION'S CUSTOMER DATA

Why do customers favour our products and services over our competitors? And vice versa? How will they do so in the future. These are questions that Master Experts are comfortable answering. Are you?

CURRENT & FUTURE ISSUES

You need to understand your organization's customers. Without a working knowledge of customer statistics – their needs, preferences, service experiences, issues and concerns, etc. – you will appear to be out of touch with the organization's primary business.

SUGGESTED ACTIVITY

- Make a point of seeking out any customer research or profiling that your organization gathers. Familiarize yourself with customers' expectations, needs, preferences and accounts of their experiences.
- Make a particular point of understanding:
  - What kinds of things customers find especially satisfying. What it is that your organization does that keeps customers coming back?
  - What kinds of things customers find dissatisfying. What threatens their loyalty or actually causes them to take their business elsewhere, common complaints, etc.
  - How customers describe their needs – both current and emerging.
- Gather a combination of quantitative (measurable) data as well as qualitative (stories and examples) data. Identify how they might inform your own team vision, priorities and provisions of advice and service.

DESIRED SITUATION

Understanding customer data will help you align your services and solutions with customer priorities. By making explicit reference to customer data, you will convey your commitment to and focus on adding value to organizational results and the customer experience.

44 LEARN YOUR ORGANIZATION'S CUSTOMER VALUE PROPOSITION

If we wish to position ourselves as Master Experts, we won't simply take the sales department's answer, or even the marketing departments take on what customers really value. We'll find a way of asking customers directly. In the end, our role is to help extend our customer value proposition.

CURRENT & FUTURE ISSUES

You need to continually refresh your sense of what it is that your customers or stakeholders value. If you do not, you will quickly lose relevance.

SUGGESTED ACTIVITY

- Although there may be a written statement outlining your organization's customer value proposition, you need to go further than merely reading those words. You need to be able to fluently and convincingly articulate precisely what it is that your organization offers to customers that they happen to find more compelling than your competitors' equivalent offers. What is it that makes them initiate and sustain a business relationship with your organization?
- You should be able to explain convincingly and precisely why your organization has a more compelling value proposition. What keenly felt needs does it address more effectively than comparative offers?
- Practise articulating how your expert function contributes to it. What is the value proposition of your function to your stakeholders? What is it that your advice and expertise allow them to achieve that is of value to them and wouldn't otherwise be possible? How precisely is it that you and your team offer them a compelling best option?
- In these times of outsourcing and technological disruption, it's important to understand that your organization most likely has alternative options to utilising your expertise, even if they don't happen to be actively considering them at present. Ensuring that you have a compelling value proposition offers you some insurance against becoming obsolete. And it also ensures that your services and advice remain relevant, on target, and good value for money. At the very least, you should be less cost-constrained.

DESIRED SITUATION

Developing and selling others on a compelling value proposition ensures that you are perceived as relevant and adding value – less susceptible to budget cuts, outsourcing, etc.

45 CONDUCT TREND ANALYSES AND DEVELOP SCENARIOS

Master Experts can see round corners. That's because they have taken global trends and considered how those trends will manifest in their own technical domain and organization.

CURRENT & FUTURE ISSUES

Without the foresight to anticipate emerging needs, issues and opportunities, experts can find themselves being reactive and playing catch-up. This means they provide minimal guidance to the organization as to how it might capitalize on favorable opportunities. If we don't have insightful contingency plans in place, we are unable to inoculate our organization or department against critical incidents and the associated ill effects.

SUGGESTED ACTIVITY

- Study meta-trends that might impact your industry and customers. As with all of these recommendations to conduct analysis, they can be performed as a solo activity or performed with other stakeholders. They can be conducted simply to prompt insight but, better still, to stimulate insight-driven actions. One popular framework for conducting such analysis is the PEST framework:
  - *Political:* what kind of developments are emerging in the regulatory arena and what implications might these have for your function, organization, industry and customers?
  - *Environmental:* As the world becomes more concerned with climate change, what implications might this have for your function, organization, industry, customers, etc?
  - *Sociological:* What kinds of trends are emerging when it comes to societal or workforce demographics. What might be the implications for your function, organization, industry, customers, etc.?
  - *Technological:* What kinds of technological innovations are emerging and what implications might these have for your function, organization, industry and customers?
- Sometimes people add Legal and Economic factors to create PESTLE.
- Specific meta-trends that you might want to consider include:
  - The rise of artificial intelligence and other technological breakthroughs (data-analytics, driverless cars, augmented reality, machine-learning, cloud computing, blockchain, increased digitally-enabled remote working, etc.)
  - Data-gathering and mining.
  - Crypto-currencies.
  - Generation Z entering the workplace.
  - The ageing population.

**DESIRED
SITUATION**

With scenario planning, the core idea is to think through which possible developments in your trend analysis are most likely to eventuate and ask 'what if ...?' Once you have explored the potential implications, you can put plans in place ahead of time either to capitalise on opportunities, immunise against risks or at least respond efficiently if they happen.

Having contingency plans in place will give you and your stakeholders some peace of mind. Putting those plans into action in the event of an envisioned scenario and offsetting emerging risks or swiftly capitalizing on opportunities will provide significant real-world advantages. You will be seen as a visionary. Thinking about the longer-term horizon rather than the work we have immediately in front of us will help you to bring more informed, strategic contributions to your work engagements as well as the planning and delivery of projects.

VALUE IMPACT

Identifies, articulates and realizes tangible ways of adding commercial or community value, demonstrating an active engagement in improving overall organizational performance.

THE THREE EXPERT ROLES OF VALUE IMPACT

OPERATIONAL VALUE CREATOR

Creating real value from incremental technical initiatives to organization-wide efficiencies.

CUSTOMER VALUE CREATOR

Creating real competitive advantage, from incremental change initiatives to breakthrough initiatives that deliver significant advantage over the competition.

COMPETITIVE ADVANTAGE CREATOR

Creating value for customers and stakeholders, from internal customer value-adds, through to external customer value breakthroughs.

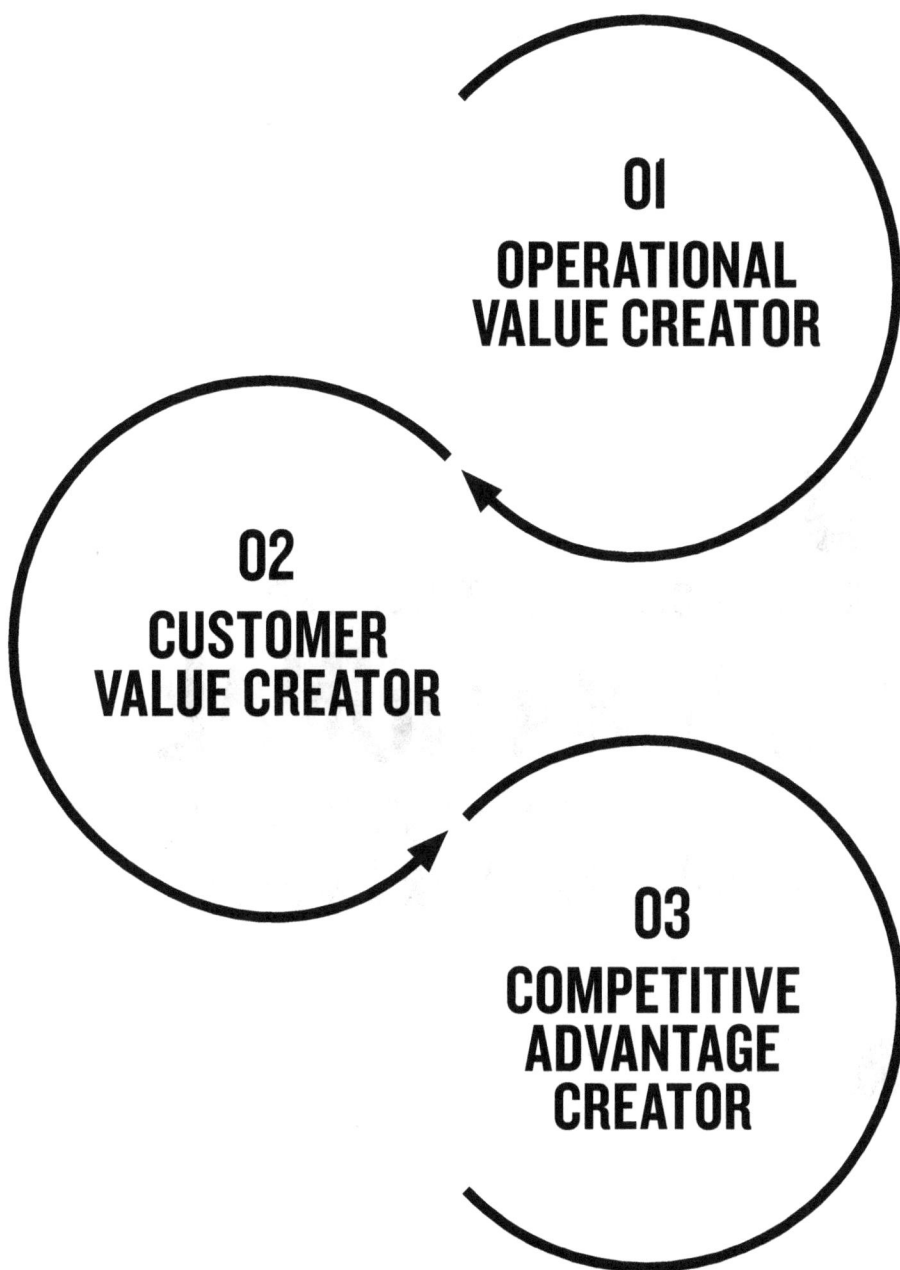

01
OPERATIONAL VALUE CREATOR

02
CUSTOMER VALUE CREATOR

03
COMPETITIVE ADVANTAGE CREATOR

01

HOW TO BECOME A MASTER EXPERT

OPERATIONAL VALUE CREATOR

CAPABAILITY: VALUE IMPACT
EXPERT ROLE: OPERATIONAL VALUE CREATOR

MASTER EXPERT	• Recommendations made on business, long-term, organisational, and strategic considerations. • Demonstrates long-term commercial reasoning when presenting ideas. • Leads visionary, improved, whole-of-business outcomes around operational transformation.
EXPERT	• Recommendations made on technical, business, medium-term, functional, and tactical considerations. • Demonstrates commercial reasoning when presenting ideas. • Delivers significantly improved functional outcomes around operational efficiency.
SPECIALIST	• Recommendations made on technical, short-term, departmental, and tactical considerations. • Rarely deploys commercial reasoning when presenting ideas. • Contributes to improvements in operational efficiency on a departmental basis.
DERAILING	• Delivers technical solutions with little connection to organizational budgets, goals, and strategic direction. • Never deploys commercial reasoning when presenting ideas. • Proposes commercially impractical ideas, shows little commercials awareness.

(46) UNDERSTAND THE ORGANIZATION'S PRIMARY METRICS AND HOW THEY ARE PERFORMING

We tend to be very focused on the metrics we use to measure our own performance but what measures does the organisation use to measure it's performance, and – here is a strategic question for Master Experts – are they the right measures?

CURRENT & FUTURE ISSUES

You need to be aware of its performance metrics that the organization, its leaders and the majority of its employees are focused on and accountable for. If you are not then then you are missing out on some significant organizational context and this will send the signal that you're not interested in organizational performance. You will be seen as another mouth to feed rather than a creator of value.

SUGGESTED ACTIVITY

- Different organizations have different approaches to collating their scorecards. In some organizations, it will purely be a financial document – targeted income compared to actual income, targeted expenses versus actual expenses, etc. In other organizations there may be a full balanced scorecard – with customer metrics, employee metrics and metrics indicating the efficiency or productivity of systems.
- In a smaller organization, you could probably just ask a senior manager if you can receive copies of the report when it is produced. Explain that your intention is to become more informed about company performance. In larger organizations, there will likely be a reporting function. They may want your manager's approval before sharing such data. Or you might find that your manager is already a recipient of this data and they can share it with you.
- Your goal in acquiring this information is to have your finger on the pulse of the organization and to identify ways in which you can create value. Is the business performing well? Is it improving, standing still or going backwards? More revenues than last year? What's driving its growth? Or what explains its declining numbers? How's profitability? How is the variance between budgeted performance and actual performance? Are there any metrics which are concerning? Which are the senior managers most focused on?

DESIRED SITUATION

Simply being in the know about the organization's performance data will have a brand enhancing effect. You will be seen as someone who cares about and is committed to lifting organizational performance. Even more significantly, familiarizing yourself with the organizational metrics will typically present opportunities for you to deploy your expertise in creating high profile value

47

EXPLICITLY APPLY COMMERCIAL REASONING WHENEVER YOU MAKE A PROPOSAL

In public sector organisations this would be community/value reasoning, but in commercial organisations the question is how will this make or save us money, or lead to more revenue or less costs. Any proposal without these questions being asked is unlikely to garner interest or support.

CURRENT & FUTURE ISSUES

You want to make proposals or recommendations that exhibit commercial reasoning. Otherwise your proposals or recommendations are unlikely to be approved or adopted, and you will be seen as impractical and out of step with reality. Proposals that don't have clearly defined benefits can't be measured, and thus their effectiveness is not realized. Proposals are most likely to be successful if their connection to the strategy of the organization are obvious to everyone – and measurable.

SUGGESTED ACTIVITY

- Next time you make a proposal or recommendation, aim to convey the anticipated payoff in commercial terms.
- If it's not obvious to you what the economic payoff would be then it won't be obvious to others either. They will just see the 'investment' you have proposed as a cost. They need to be made aware of the potential value – the return on the investment. Is what you're proposing likely to have a positive impact on a key organizational metric? Will it save costs? Improve efficiency? Increase customer loyalty – or at least reduce complaints? Can you predict which metric should move? By how much? And is there a way of monetizing the value of that uplift or saving?
- Measure any uplifts or savings and produce an impact report post-implementation. This will convey that you can be a trusted steward of organizational resources – that you have delivered the promised return on investment.

DESIRED SITUATION

Exhibiting commercial reasoning will positively influence your brand. You'll be viewed as commercially savvy – relevant, central to strategic thinking and implementation. More of your proposals or recommendations will be adopted. You will have increased clout.

48 RIGOROUSLY BENCHMARK YOUR SERVICES VERSUS YOUR COMPETITORS

Many experts work in shared services environments. How do you know you are doing "better" than the rival shared services team across the road at your competitors?

CURRENT & FUTURE ISSUES

We seek to avoid working in a bubble – believing that we are delivering wonderful work without really having any sensible benchmark to help us understand just how well we are performing. We are seeking to be able to establish the quality of our work, and our market leadership (if this is indeed the reality), or argue for changes in resource allocations if we can demonstrate we are falling behind competitors.

SUGGESTED ACTIVITY

- Whatever your expert realm, the organizations with whom you compete almost certainly have similar roles. Ask yourself – how well do you know, for certain, without hubris, how well your service compares with that provided by your counterparts in rival organizations?
- Some expert functions have simple measures of competitive performance – for example, sales have revenue, yield, and market share metrics to enable them to see how well they are performing against sales teams in rival organizations. But many experts employed in shared or enabling service functions don't (and many experts reside in these fields). You need to build a capability to understand how well you are doing competitively.
- You might start with talking to employees who have just joined your organization from rivals. They may be able to give you a clear opinion on, for example, how good the IT service is compared with their previous employer or whether HR has a good reputation and service delivery model. Or whether facilities management get stuff fixed quickly, or not.
- You should search for other signs and symbols of how well the "other team" is doing in comparison to you. Keep an eye out for any presentations from officers of competitive organizations who operate in your special field, and attend those presentations and conferences to see what they have to say.
- If you can find the budget, many research organizations offer paid benchmarking services that can enable you to audit your departmental performance.

DESIRED SITUATION

The true measure of best practice is that you are providing services to a quality level and at a price point that is at least as good as your competitors, if not better. You gain true credibility if this is the measure by which you and your craft hold yourself accountable, rather than just getting things done on time and to budget.

49

VOLUNTEER FOR A CROSS-ORGANIZATION PROJECT

Master Experts interact with all parts of the organization, not just those colleagues in their own technical domain. The fastest way to build internal networks, and experience how other departments work and think, is to join a cross-organisational project.

CURRENT & FUTURE ISSUES

Cross-organizational projects enable us to build broader networks of experts in other functions which have benefits well beyond the life of the specific project. These projects also expose us to diverse thinking and perspectives that enable us to understand the broader organization – and how it works – better than just staying in our technical comfort zone. Involvement in such projects stops us being isolated and insular in our thinking and experiences.

SUGGESTED ACTIVITY

- Explore which projects are likely to be coming up, what sort of contributions the leaders of those projects are looking for, and how members of the project are selected.
- Have a conversation with your manager about wishing to be involved in such projects. Seek their recommendation and sponsorship.
- Once appointed to a project, make sure you set yourself clear goals for taking on the extra work and responsibility. Set measurable SMART goals for how you hope the project will assist your development as a Master Expert.
- Make sure that you devote an appropriate amount of time in order deliver on your promises and make your contribution to the project memorable for all the right reasons.
- Adopt a 'two hats' approach to your contribution – and make sure that you think about which hat you are wearing. The first hat will be your default thinking – coming at problems from the perspective of your domain specialism (whether IT, or risk, or HR, etc.) The second hat is the project hat – the whole of organization thinking. One of the purposes of being on the project is to develop this whole of organization perspective. In terms of advancing to Master Expert, it is a critical skill to develop.
- Make sure you conduct – as a project team – a Post Project Review, and discuss with your colleagues what went well, and what could have been done better. These are lessons for everyone to take into the next project experience. If you see the PPR not taking place, take the lead and make it happen. Everyone will not initially thank you for creating yet another meeting for them to attend, but they will thank you once a good review has taken place and everyone can take away the lessons.

DESIRED SITUATION

A greater appreciation of how the organization works outside your department. A greater appreciation of the diversity of viewpoints across the organization. An enhanced and broader stakeholder map and network. An enhanced personal brand.

50 SPEND MORE TIME "OUT IN THE WILD"

Experts who tell us they don't have time are really telling us they have no idea how to prioritise. They can't prioritise because they can't see the big picture – the issues that really matter to the whole organisation. Getting wild is the only way to get this perspective.

CURRENT & FUTURE ISSUES

Most experts are very busy and their focus tends to be almost exclusively on doing work and having meetings with others talking about work done and work to do. This leaves no time to spend time out in the wider organization observing how our work is impacting other colleagues and customers, and understanding what the impact (positive and negative) is of our work.

SUGGESTED ACTIVITY

- Convince yourself that spending time out in the wider organization ("in the wild") is not a waste of time but is actually a mechanism to stop us wasting time. Time spent with stakeholders and colleagues who depend on our work and expertise helps us differentiate requests that are important from those which are not. It helps us prioritise based on real user needs, rather than the needs of those who are shouting loudest and longest.
- Convince yourself that you are welcome – and discover this yourself when you actually arrive and see colleagues are delighted to see you, and see you being directly and personally interested in the challenges they face every day and concerned about them.
- Steal yourself to listen and not problem solve. Spending time out in the organization is an intelligence gathering exercise, not a problem-solving trip.
- Spend time with real people not just the leaders.
- Prioritise this over other activities (the hardest thing to do), because you will be discovering what matters and what doesn't, and that enables you to provide help where it is most needed.

DESIRED SITUATION

Greater familiarisation with what is happening in the real world, and how you might be able to positively impact colleagues and customers. Less dependence on intermediaries who might simply be prioritising their own agendas. You will have seen it yourself and be able to challenge. Greater understanding of where value might be created, rather than simply responding to work requests from unknown stakeholders.

02

HOW TO BECOME A MASTER EXPERT

CUSTOMER VALUE CREATOR

CAPABILITY: VALUE IMPACT
EXPERT ROLE: CUSTOMER VALUE CREATOR

MASTER EXPERT	• Recommendations made deliver long-term product/service benefits to the organization's customers. • Demonstrates a strong commitment to understanding and reacting to changing customer needs today and in the future. • Routinely delivers new value to internal customers.
EXPERT	• Recommendations made deliver short-term product/service benefits to some of the organization's customers. • Demonstrates an understanding of current customer needs. • Responds effectively to requests for added value from internal customers.
SPECIALIST	• Main focus is on internal customers • Will consider internal customer feedback when making recommendations around technical solutions. • Reacts positively to requests for new solutions.
DERAILING	• Is focused on internal immediate internal customers. • Demonstrates no awareness of customer needs. • Advocates doing it like we've always done it, pushing back on requests for innovative solutions.

(51) # DEVELOP CUSTOMER-CENTRIC REASONING

Whether it is your immediate stakeholders (and managers) or the removed stakeholders (and organizational customers), we are living in a very dynamic working environment where what was perceived as good value by our customers last year won't be considered the required higher standard this year. We have to create extra value by delivering more with less on a constant basis. The easiest way to do this is to ensure we really understand what today's customers, and tomorrow's, will want and consider valuable, and how is that different from the past.

CURRENT & FUTURE ISSUES

You need to provide a positive benefit for customers as an outcome of what you're doing. Otherwise, you'll be competing with other cost centres for a small piece of organizational funding – and your solutions and services may be of questionable importance. Also to avoid doing things for the wrong reasons that departments usually do things "because we've always done it this way" or "this is the easiest way to do it". In both of these instances, you are focusing on activities and the how, not the why.

SUGGESTED ACTIVITY

- Position all recommendations – where possible – in terms of the positive impact that they will have on the organization's customers. To do this, you will have to research how you can credibly create line of sight to positive customer impacts. You'll need to know how customers define value – and how your contributions positively impact the value chain between you and the customer.
- Consider what other groups of customers exist that are different from yours but in adjacent sectors, and look at who is providing new customer impacts and value in that sector.

DESIRED SITUATION

Experts who employ a strong customer centric rationale will be seen as strategic players, providing business-critical services and have a higher proportion of their recommendations and proposals adopted.

52 LEVERAGE BREAKTHROUGH IDEAS IN OTHER INDUSTRIES TO CREATE NEW CUSTOMER VALUE

AirBnb realised that when people visit a place, they want to experience it as a local not a visitor. How can we take this idea and apply it to our organization, our customers, our colleagues? This is the Master Expert art of leveraging breakthrough ideas elsewhere.

CURRENT & FUTURE ISSUES

To be the first in your industry or specialty to adopt new ideas that have worked in other industries. You'll be at the vanguard of creating new value and competitive advantage. To avoid being surprised by new customer requirements, which are often generated by new services and features they are being offered in other parts of life.

SUGGESTED ACTIVITY

- Leverage wider reading and broader perspectives.
- Become a student of the 'breakthrough'. Don't worry about the personal stardust associated with entrepreneurs who are changing markets, but explore what thinking got them to the 'new' and the 'breakthrough'. How might that thinking and those concepts apply to your organization? This thinking and analysis are the prelude to action.
- Consider which internal stakeholders have the most to gain from any similar breakthrough in your organization. Approach them with a view to starting a pilot, or some way of testing the new ideas in your environment. Work on small and iterative best practice.
- Carefully manage expectations – earlier deployments are unlikely to fit. It is the constant refinement of how these new ideas apply to your organizations that will get you there in the end.

DESIRED SITUATION

Experts who deploy this innovative approach can expect to have several detractors early on. You might also expect to be challenged constantly about why this new idea might work until you stumble through trial and error on a breakthrough application of the breakthrough idea. Then they will be asking for your next idea, and invitations to strategic meetings at senior level will be commonplace.

(53) PROMOTE AND UTILISE SCENARIO PLANNING TO VISUALIZE BEST PRACTICE

Using eclectic teams to help us scenario plan - for the future creates fun, creates focus, and shines the light on which parts of our work add value, and which don't.

CURRENT & FUTURE ISSUES

Scenario planning, if used in a future-focused situation, helps you begin to imagine the opportunities and challenges of your role, the value you add and what it might look like in two or three years' time. It helps you develop a viewpoint on what next practice looks like.

Scenario planning avoids unwelcome surprises.

We want to ensure our thinking is current and future-proofed.

SUGGESTED ACTIVITY

- Catch up on the latest techniques for scenario planning, and adopt a process that seems right for your team.
- Consider which colleagues to involve in the process. This is a team sport.
- Be clear on what you are trying to achieve. You want to know what might happen in the best and worst situation, and then start taking into account these assumptions in your medium-term planning.
- Consider adopting a strategy canvas approach to your planning – referencing Blue Ocean Strategy (W. Chan Kim and Renée Mauborgne) - this is a great book for thinking about strategy.
- You may find that to conduct scenario planning properly, you'll need to engage with specialists from other departments to give you a holistic view.

DESIRED SITUATION

If you undertake this properly, you can expect some insights as to the rate of change (likely to be faster than you think) and the scope of change (likely to be wider than you might have imagined). This helps you to prepare better for the future demands of your customers. You might find that several long-held beliefs and planning assumptions are challenged - yours and other people's. This tells you that you are spending valuable time, because challenging sacred cows is what scenario planning and customer value creation is all about.

03

HOW TO BECOME A MASTER EXPERT

COMPETITIVE ADVANTAGE CREATOR

CAPABAILITY: VALUE IMPACT
EXPERT ROLE: COMPETITVE ADVANTAGE CREATOR

MASTER EXPERT	• Actively shapes and refines solutions to deliver significant business impact. • Focuses on future needs of the organisation to extend competitive position. • Makes recommendations that deliver against long-term strategic goals and competitive advantage.
EXPERT	• Actively shapes solutions to add technical and organizational advantage. • Focuses on near term initiatives to maintain competitive position. • Makes recommendations that deliver against immediate organizational priorities.
SPECIALIST	• Shapes technical solutions for departmental improvements. • Applies focus to immediate action list. • Makes recommendations for small, short-term, incremental improvements.
DERAILING	• Applies focus from a purely technical perspective without consideration to broader organizational goals or competitive position. • Is reactive rather than proactive in making any recommendations.

(54) LEVERAGE BREAKTHROUGH IDEAS FROM OTHER INDUSTRIES

Even if we want to maintain market position and not extend it, we'll have to do things differently in the future. What things? What ideas that are taking hold in other industries might work in ours?

CURRENT & FUTURE ISSUES

Future success for the organization is likely to depend on doing something different to current practice. The question becomes how you and your colleagues generate these new ideas.

SUGGESTED ACTIVITY

- Become a student of successful innovations and breakthrough practices in other industry sectors. Seek to understand how the innovations are delivering competitive advantage for the early adopters. Ask to what extent could and should these ideas be implemented in your sector.
- While it is easier to understand trends occurring in adjacent sectors, most wild ideas are likely to come from completely unrelated industries.
- Attend events outside your sector expertise, to see how other expert groups are addressing the dynamic changes happening in their sector.
- Study global trends that will impact your sector – such as personalization, digital business etc. – and be a thought leader in how these trends will impact your organization.

DESIRED SITUATION

Broader thinking about the future shape of how your expertise will be applied (and needed) in your organization. New insights into what your customers will expect from your organization in the future. Building status in the organization as a thought leader who is future focused. Expect to get invited to more meetings where future strategy and customer value creation is discussed because you can make a meaningful contribution.

55 HANG WITH CUSTOMER FACING TEAMS

Spending time with people who spend time with customers is transformative if you have never done it before. You'll find out things that change the way you do your job.

CURRENT & FUTURE ISSUES

Avoid seeing issues only from your specialist point of view. Be aware of how issues look from other team perspectives in your organization. Cross-pollinization of ideas between different teams leads to greater diversity of thought and ideas.

SUGGESTED ACTIVITY

- Make a case with customer facing teams that you will be able to serve them better by spending time observing what they do and how they interact with customers. Over time, build trust so they know that you're safe to take to customer meetings and other interactions.
- Be clear on what you are trying to achieve. Develop an intimate knowledge of how things work currently, and why they are currently designed that way. This will enable you to be better able to think through incremental changes that will redefine customer value.
- Develop an 'insights' process with customer facing teams. Ask to be included in all research and feedback and NPS scores etc. and make a point of reading and then discussing this data with customer facing teams. What do they think the data means? What are they doing about it?

DESIRED SITUATION

To create a collective team culture of collaboration and sharing rather than separateness. Not only will you be seen as an exceptional leader in your contribution to bringing teams together, but you will gain a reputation of developing and engaging high performing, collaborative and inclusive teams.

56 HANG WITH CUSTOMERS

An extension of the last growth initiative, never mind spending time with intermediaries. Get out and meet real customers.

CURRENT & FUTURE ISSUES

Avoid seeing issues only from what your customer-facing teams tell you – they have agendas and bias too. Be aware of how issues look from customers of your organization.

SUGGESTED ACTIVITY

- Make a case with customers that you will be able to serve them better by spending time observing what they do and how they interact with your organization. Over time, build trust so they know that you're safe to talk to and share insights.
- Understand that customer-facing teams will worry about you spending time with customers without them. Understand what they are worried about, and make sure you don't cross policy or trust lines. Help them understand that responses from customers are necessarily influenced by who else is in the room.
- Be clear on what you are trying to achieve. Make sure you are asking customers about other choices they have, and why they choose your organization, and why in the future they may choose alternative suppliers.

DESIRED SITUATION

Being in direct contact with external customers for some experts is a very large leap, but it enables you to speak with authority about what customers are doing, thinking and valuing in your organization's services and products without having to rely on others. This completely changes the status you have – and the strategic value you can create – in your organization.

CHANGE IMPACT

Acts as a change catalyst and leads change initiatives effectively.

THE THREE EXPERT ROLES OF CHANGE IMPACT

CHANGE SUPPORTER

Champions productive change, avoiding a closed and negative mindset, instead embracing change constructively and positively.

CHANGE CATALYST

Generating organizational change initiatives and being the catalyst to making things happen.

CHANGE LEADER

Leading change initiatives where required, inspiring and managing teams through change.

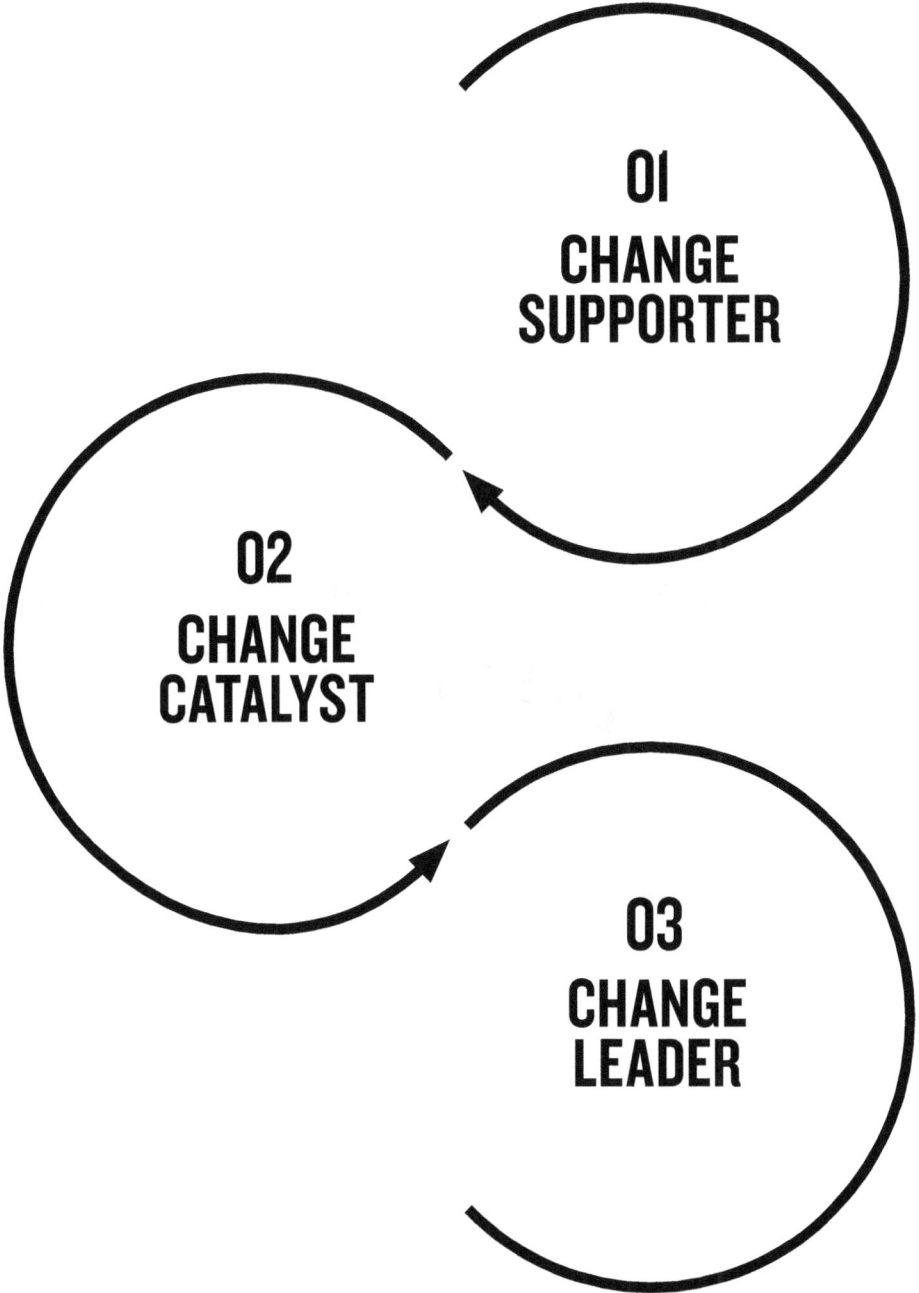

01
CHANGE
SUPPORTER

02
CHANGE
CATALYST

03
CHANGE
LEADER

01

HOW TO BECOME A MASTER EXPERT

CHANGE
SUPPORTER

CAPABAILITY: CHANGE IMPACT
EXPERT ROLE: CHANGE SUPPORTER

MASTER EXPERT	• Promotes and models a positive change culture. • Able to envisage and articulate organizational change benefits.
EXPERT	• Models a supportive mindset towards change. • Able to envisage and articulate departmental change benefits.
SPECIALIST	• Models a developing ability to embrace and participate in change. • Abel to envisage and articulate individual changes benefits.
DERAILING	• Closed mindset towards change. • Immediate resistance when change is proposed. • Dismissive of change initiatives publicly.

(57) BE A PROPONENT, NOT A CRITIC

Because we've seen it all go wrong, and be so badly handled in the past, it's easy to be a negative voice. It is much harder to research the reason why, keep an open mind, believe that this time it really could be different. Real influence is being seen to be on the bus but suggesting short cuts. Zero influence is being seen as the usual, "it will end in tears" subject matter expert.

CURRENT & FUTURE ISSUES

Respond positively to change. Do not automatically oppose it or criticize it. Experts who respond negatively to change often end up alienating and marginalizing themselves, getting others offside (particularly the senior people who have initiated the change) and sometimes entirely sabotaging or undermining change initiatives.

SUGGESTED ACTIVITY

- Next time there's a change, even if you feel sceptical and resistant, aim to be as open-minded as possible. Proactively seek out the reasons for the change – even if they haven't been articulated fluently to you. There's every likelihood that others may not have perfectly articulated the case for change. Rather than taking this as a justification for adopting an oppositional stance, adopt a constructive mindset. You may be able to help strengthen the case.
- There may be times when the change being proposed is a flawed idea that would benefit from being appropriately challenged. In this case, challenge constructively.
- Be an early adopter and supporter of the change.

DESIRED SITUATION

Becoming a constructive participant in the change process will convey to others that you are an improvement-oriented, responsive corporate citizen. You will be seen as someone they can depend on to use their influence constructively.

58 VOLUNTEER TO BE A CHANGE CHAMPION

If we believe the role of Master Experts is to drive innovation that will inspire tomorrow's products and service, we need to make change our middle name. That means getting out and experiencing just how hard it can be.

CURRENT & FUTURE ISSUES

You need to lead from the front, even if it wasn't you who initiated the change. If you don't, you could miss the opportunity to play a constructive role in helping shepherd others through change. If you don't grasp these opportunities you might be seen as just another non-differentiated passenger to be brought on the journey – rather than an active crew member committed to the realisation of organizational objectives.

SUGGESTED ACTIVITY

- Volunteer your services as a change champion when the next change initiative kicks off. Participate in shaping a compelling case for and narrative around the change. A case for change is typically grounded in one of two factors (or sometimes both):
  - Illustrating the problems of making no change.
  - Describing the benefits of changing – a compelling future state.
- Actively seek to engage colleagues and other stakeholders in accepting and embracing the change.

DESIRED SITUATION

Becoming an active change champion will not necessarily accelerate the implementation – and benefits realization – of change initiatives. But it will elevate your brand to one of being a trusted adviser to business leaders and a trusted friend to colleagues.

59 UNDERSTAND (AND DEVELOP) YOUR OWN CHANGE AGILITY

We all have different default settings, based on personality and experiences, when it comes to our ability to embrace change.

CURRENT & FUTURE ISSUES

Build our capability to assess change initiatives on their merits, and support people through change as an informal leader. Not allowing our personal biases, either as a change cynic or a change advocate, to determine our response to change.

SUGGESTED ACTIVITY

- Explore your change history, considering what your first impressions have been when change has been imposed on you. What does it tell you about your default settings?
- Consider why your default settings are as they are. Are they a function of your personality, or are they the result of the experiences you have had with change?
- Undertake a profile that helps you understand how you react to change.
- Develop a set of questions that you can ask neutrally about any change initiative. These might include exploring the rationale behind the change, whether no change at all is really an option (it very often isn't), and to what extent the change will assist your organization execute its strategy or purpose. Keep an open mind about the change until you can answer these questions in an informed way.

DESIRED SITUATION

Building a personal brand that is open to change. Being seen as someone who can help expedite the change process, rather than a blocker, or an enthusiastic exuberant supporter of change without consideration of the issues.

60

BE A STUDENT OF THE CHANGE CURVE

Typically, many people experience a range of emotions when disruptive changes are announced in their organization. These are often described on the change curve (see Appendix iv), which is based on the stages of grief people feel when they lose a loved one.

CURRENT & FUTURE ISSUES

To avoid being unreasonably dismissive of emotional responses from colleagues undergoing change; the ability to understand why they are feeling as they are. Being in an informed position to help colleagues successfully cope with change.

SUGGESTED ACTIVITY

- Study the change curve. Understand the different stages, and how these may cause different personal behaviors from colleagues.
- Consider your own and others' responses to change.
- Consider what support colleagues need, depending on what stage of the change curve they are at. Offer this support at the appropriate time.

DESIRED SITUATION

Building a personal brand that is open to change. Being seen as someone who can help expedite the change process, rather than a blocker or an enthusiastic exuberant supporter of change without consideration of the issues.

02

HOW TO BECOME A MASTER EXPERT

CHANGE CATALYST

CAPABAILITY: CHANGE IMPACT
EXPERT ROLE: CHANGE CATALYST

MASTER EXPERT	• Acts as a catalyst for change, sets the change agenda. • Continuously seeks better ways of executing and adding value across the organisation. • Objectively questions enterprise and market assumptions, and challenges the status quo. • Anticipates opportunities for disruption and to disrupt.
EXPERT	• Identifies and promotes departmental change initiatives. • Continuously seeks better ways of executing and adding value within function. • Objectively questions departmental assumptions, and challenges the status quo.
SPECIALIST	• Identifies and promotes individual change opportunities.
DERAILING	• Comfortable with the status quo. • Rarely considers the case for change.

61 SEEK OUT WHAT'S NOT WORKING

Seasoned experts have a tendency to be jaundiced about what isn't working in their organization – often blaming it on "management". Master Experts dive in, trying to understand why things aren't working and proactively doing something about it.

CURRENT & FUTURE ISSUES

To find meaningful and actionable ways to do more with less. As a change catalyst, we need to seek out these opportunities regularly. We want to ensure our processes and knowledge do not go stale, which would require others to generate change suggestions.

SUGGESTED ACTIVITY

- Listen hard to what colleagues and stakeholders are saying about the challenges they face in the workplace and in serving customers. Very often meaningful and actionable changes are suggested by these comments.
- Get curious. Take the time to try and understand why processes and systems are as they are. For how long have these processes been the same? How might they be improved? Is the latest technology and systems thinking being applied to the issue? What are the barriers to change and improvement? Are they legitimate barriers or signs that colleagues simply don't want to change?
- Get competitive. What are your strengths and weaknesses against competitors (or best practice in the public sector)? How are they delivering their competitive advantage? What would be required of us not just to catch up (i.e. achieve current best practice) but leap ahead (i.e. next practice)?

DESIRED SITUATION

More ideas will be generated by taking this investigative and curious approach. You will establish a reputation for good ideas that deliver competitive advantage to your organization.

62

SEEK OUT WHAT NEW THINGS ARE WORKING FOR OTHERS

The problem we, or our organisation has, is statistically unlikely to be unique. Who else has already fixed it for their organisation, and how do we leverage that experience?

CURRENT & FUTURE ISSUES

To find meaningful and actionable ways to do things differently, building on others' successes. As a change catalyst, we need to seek out these opportunities regularly.

We want to leverage breakthroughs and innovative ideas others have deployed and as quickly as possible, gain these benefits by deploying them in our own department, division, organization or industry.

SUGGESTED ACTIVITY

- Ask internal colleagues in other departments and divisions what they are doing differently and why, and consider which improvements might work in your own department. This might be an immediate initiative, and then become a regular (say quarterly) chat between different groups. You should be ready to share improvements you have made.
- When seeking feedback, insist on suggested improvements. Make suggesting an improvement mandatory. Don't settle for "I can't think of anything". When really pushed, customers and clients can almost always think of some small thing that can be improved.
- Aggressively benchmark. At Expertunity, we always ask our clients to tell us what other suppliers (not necessarily in our field) are doing better than us. Most of our productivity and service improvements come from asking these questions.

DESIRED SITUATION

The constant quest for insights that increase the effectiveness of our function is a brand attribute that quickly gets recognized and rewarded. The ability to deliver even small changes and improvements to service and product regularly sets you apart from those experts who rest on their laurels.

63
APPLY THE
10 PER CENT RULE

Incrementally improving what we do is much easier than trying to reinvent a process or solution from scratch. Incremental innovation often leads to greater productivity gains than hothouse sessions.

CURRENT & FUTURE ISSUES

To build a constant learning environment, growing incremental innovation as part of business as usual settings. Ensure that we – and our immediate colleagues – don't rest on existing knowledge and process.

SUGGESTED ACTIVITY

- Introduce the concept of the 10 per cent rule. On a monthly basis, you consider how the work done last month might be improved by 10 per cent this month. This might involve reducing effort by 10 per cent for the same result, or an extra 10 per cent in productivity for the same effort, or a bit of both.
- This might involve a monthly meeting – for perhaps 30 minutes – to discuss ideas on how improvement can be made. Typically, the improvements identified are small items, but cumulatively they make a big difference.

DESIRED SITUATION

You might be surprised at how many small incremental improvements are identifiable if there is a will to find them, and a process where colleagues come ready to contribute. One product of this initiative is that Kaizen – the Japanese term for continuous improvement – becomes part of business as usual.

03

HOW TO BECOME A MASTER EXPERT

CHANGE
LEADER

CAPABAILITY: CHANGE IMPACT
EXPERT ROLE: CHANGE LEADER

MASTER EXPERT	• Leads with insight—provides direction and institutes effective strategies to constructively engage people in change. • Understands how organizational stakeholders may be impacted by change. • Proactively assists others in dealing with change.
EXPERT	• Helps execute change initiatives with professionalism and commitment. • Understands how departmental stakeholders may be impacted by change. • Assists others in dealing with change.
SPECIALIST	• Contributes dutifully towards change initiative. • Raises concerns diplomatically and objectively. • Seeks to manage self through change effectively.
DERAILING	• Actively fights change initiatives—plays a blocking role. • Reacts subjectively and emotionally to change initiatives.

(64) PRACTISE EFFECTIVE CHANGE MANAGEMENT NEXT TIME YOU ARE INITIATING A CHANGE

Change is a process – well executed and people buy in. Poorly executed and people resist. Which strategy will you adopt?

CURRENT & FUTURE ISSUES

To be a change management leader, you need to anticipate how stakeholders will be impacted by any changes and how they will react. If you do not do this, you will face much more resistance to the smooth and timely execution of your plans. This may in turn detrimentally impact – or at least delay – any benefits from your change initiative.

SUGGESTED ACTIVITY

- Recognize that the change will impact others. Conduct some prior analysis of which stakeholders will be impacted and how. Consider how you'll position the rationale for the change in a fully informative and compelling fashion. Facilitate a two-way discussion with stakeholders to hear and resolve their questions and concerns. Plan implementation carefully to identify and deliver quick wins.
- Refer Appendix v for John Kotter's 8 Step Change Model which further outlines various elements of effective change management.

DESIRED SITUATION

Developing and implementing effective change management plans will likely result in more successful change implementation. You will have earlier and more favorable responses from affected stakeholders, less resistance, smoother implementation and earlier and fuller realization of benefits.

65 PROACTIVELY DEVELOP A STAKEHOLDER COMMUNICATION AND ENGAGEMENT PLAN

Many change processes map technical steps and forget about the human ones. Master Experts are expert at engaging all stakeholders throughout the whole process.

CURRENT & FUTURE ISSUES

At the heart of a change management plan there should be a deliberate process to identify all affected stakeholders and to understand how to best communicate with and engage them. If there is no effective stakeholder engagement and communications, change initiators face resistance, which will inhibit the implementation of the change initiative and its benefits.

SUGGESTED ACTIVITY

- Develop a stakeholder communication and action plan. It should be informed by what kind of commitment the change initiative needs from each stakeholder group, each group's anticipated probable reaction to the change, and identify specific personalized selling points to get their buy-in. Use the framework in Appendix vi to help you think through and develop the plan.
- Build specific storytelling narratives that enable you to pitch your ideas to stakeholder groups in a way which will appeal to them, matching their long-term needs to the change being recommended.

DESIRED SITUATION

When stakeholders are effectively engaged, they will respond more warmly to change initiatives. They will display less resistance, which will make change implementation easier, less drawn out and painful – realizing benefits sooner and more fully.

66 USE EMPATHY TO ENGAGE STAKEHOLDERS IN CHANGE INITIATIVES

One reason why most stakeholders initially resist change is that they don't believe their concerns have been heard or understood. As Master Experts, we have a large role to play in making sure this common mistake is avoided.

CURRENT & FUTURE ISSUES

You need to show empathy with your stakeholders' fears or concerns over how the change will affect them. If you don't you will seem uncaring and indifferent, which will result in increased resistance to change initiatives, slowing or impeding implementation and any benefits of the change. Bear in mind that stakeholders may have valid views and suggestions that need to be taken into account by the change leaders.

SUGGESTED ACTIVITY

- When you notice stakeholders resisting a change initiative, even if you're not the owner of the initiative, take responsibility for empathizing with their questions, concerns and reservations.
- Make sure you understand the difference between empathy (listening and understanding their concerns) and sympathy (agreeing with their concerns).
- Have conversations with stakeholders about the change process – what has worked for them before, and what hasn't. Some concerns will be about the way change is handled rather than the actual change itself.
- Coach your team and your stakeholders to be accepting of the change and to embracing a compelling view of the future post change implementation.
- Shape the implementation plan where possible in such a way that their concerns and misgivings are addressed. Encourage them to think and express themselves positively about the change.

DESIRED SITUATION

Responding to others' concerns with empathy will help them feel understood. It will also help alleviate their concerns, reducing resistance and allowing people to constructively engage with the change initiative.

67

BUILD TAILORED ENGAGEMENT STRATEGIES FOR EACH STAKEHOLDER GROUP

The world is moving towards personalization and customization, and leading change is no exception. One message fits all went out last century.

CURRENT & FUTURE ISSUES

Address each stakeholder group's concerns. Frame the rationale or benefits in ways relevant to them. A one-size-fits-all style of communication when seeking to engage stakeholders in change initiatives rarely hits the mark – you run the risk of their not buying in.

SUGGESTED ACTIVITY

- Actively work with change catalysts and initiators to develop an engagement strategy for each type of key stakeholder. Help them to conduct a stakeholder analysis – anticipating likely sentiments and responses.
- Brainstorm and propose insightful ways to foster positive engagement. Volunteer to drive crucial aspects of the communications.

DESIRED SITUATION

A tailored engagement plan for each stakeholder group increases the likelihood of fostering the requisite levels of commitment. This will result in swifter and smoother implementation and benefits realisation.

PART 3

THE
RELATIONSHIP
DOMAIN

STAKEHOLDER ENGAGEMENT

Builds and maintains mutually rewarding stakeholder relationships across a variety of internal and external stakeholder groups.

THE THREE EXPERT ROLES OF STAKEHOLDER ENGAGEMENT

INTERNAL NETWORKER

Developing a large and diverse network of stakeholders and colleagues across the organization, both local and global.

EXTERNAL NETWORKER

Developing a high-quality external network which is multi-lens and transformational.

NETWORK MANAGER

Effective and efficient at managing and maintaining a large network of colleagues and stakeholders and being proactive and strategic in doing so.

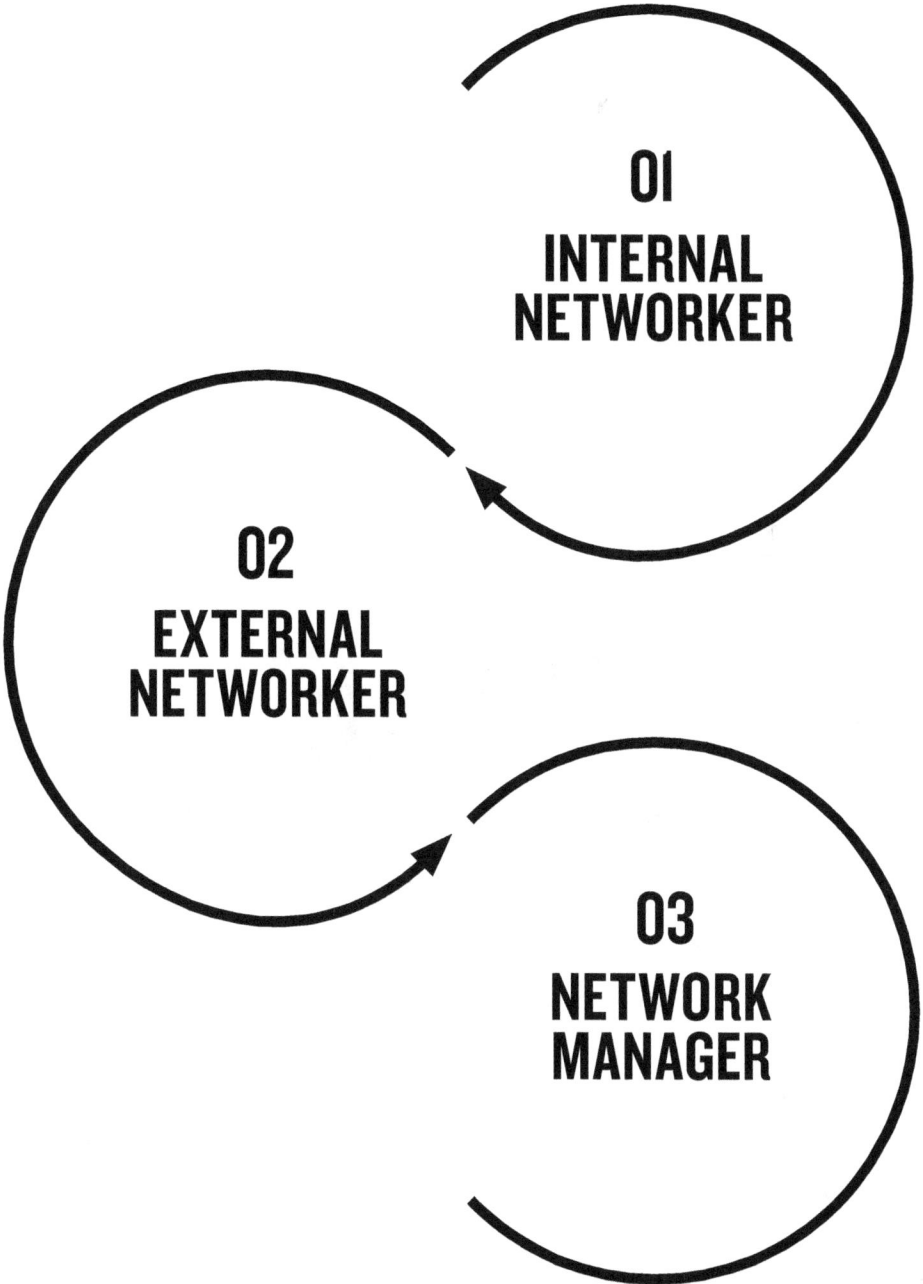

01
INTERNAL
NETWORKER

02
EXTERNAL
NETWORKER

03
NETWORK
MANAGER

01

HOW TO BECOME A MASTER EXPERT

INTERNAL NETWORKER

CAPABILITY: STAKEHOLDER ENGAGEMENT
EXPERT ROLE: INTERNAL NETWORKER

MASTER EXPERT

- Proactively builds and manages a network of effective relationships across the organization.
- Demonstrates a strong grasp of current and emerging needs of key immediate and removed stakeholders across the organisation.
- Consistently satisfies and exceeds stakeholder needs.
- Strategically prioritizes time and attention between the relationships that are important to the current mandate, and may inform future mandates.

EXPERT

- Builds and manages a network of effective relationships within their immediate operational domain.
- Demonstrates a strong grasp of current needs of key immediate stakeholders across the organisation, and is proactive in understanding all needs.
- Consistently satisfies stakeholder needs.
- Prioritizing time & attention on the relationships that are most important to current mandate.

SPECIALIST

- Manages a small but growing network of relationships directly related to current mandate.
- Demonstrates knowledge of the needs communicated by key immediate stakeholders, and is reactive to these specific needs.
- Spends time as directed by incoming mandates from stakeholders.

DERAILING

- Operates within a limited and exclusive network, maintaining relationships that are personally useful.
- Takes a transactional, self-centred view; viewing relationships as a means of getting things done and focusing on personal needs.
- May miss less obvious stakeholders, or be operating with an outdated understanding of needs.

68 GET ON THE FRONT FOOT WITH NETWORKING

Operating in a bubble, or a silo, means experts perpetuate the myth that they aren't interested in what the rest of the organization is doing. Master Experts actively network for intelligence gathering and relationship building.

CURRENT & FUTURE ISSUES

Reach out to initiate engagement with key stakeholders. This will result in a more active relationship and higher visibility of their needs. It will also make you more visible, and give you a greater appreciation of what is going on in the rest of the organization.

SUGGESTED ACTIVITY

- Identify an important stakeholder who you have yet to build any substantial connection with. There might possibly be a stakeholder with whom you and they already have a connection who might introduce you.
- Explain your intentions to the intermediate stakeholder: "You and I have been working together effectively for some time now. It also appears that you have a good working relationship with (target stakeholder). I would like to get to know them better with a view to forging a closer working relationship in order to achieve (valued organizational objective). Would you be happy to introduce me?"
- Your goal is to get a meeting in their diary – perhaps 30 minutes over coffee – to ask them about their goals and challenges and see if there's any value to be gleaned by more collaboration. State your intentions upfront: "I see you as an important stakeholder but am mindful that I have a limited understanding of the direction you're taking, the priority challenges you face and what me and my team can do to be of service. Would you mind if we spent a little time exploring that?"
- Listen. Take notes. Ask questions. And also take the opportunity to briefly explain how your team works. Explore any obvious opportunities to work more collaboratively. If there's something you can immediately do to add value – and you have the bandwidth and commitment to ensure you deliver – offer it as a gesture of goodwill. At the conclusion of the meeting, thank them for their time and, if appropriate, explore when a follow up meeting might make sense.

DESIRED SITUATION

Over time you will build more relationships with stakeholders and expand your internal network. You will foster goodwill, increase collaboration levels, and develop greater insight into stakeholders' needs.

69 CONDUCT A STAKEHOLDER ANALYSIS

Those who excel at stakeholder engagement have a structured and periodic process to ensure that they are spending time with the right stakeholders for the right reasons on the right work.

CURRENT & FUTURE ISSUES

To understand your stakeholders' needs and preferences. If you don't do this there's a possibility that you will be engaging with them purely at a functional level with little or no insight as to what really makes them tick. This can cause tensions or, more often, missed opportunities to better collaborate or satisfy each other's needs.

SUGGESTED ACTIVITY

- Conduct a proactive and periodic needs analysis of all your important stakeholders using the template in Appendix vi. Use the insights gained to evaluate where your services are most relevant and valuable. Where necessary, realign your solutions, processes and priorities.
- You might find as you work your way through the form that there are numerous questions where you're not 100 per cent sure that your answers regarding their perspective match how they would answer the same question. These might be good questions to ask them when you next have an opportunity:
  - Purpose – What do we want from the relationship? What do we need from each other? This can include both functional requirements, such as: "I need you to provide me with such and such data to include in the monthly report" – and psychological expectations such as: "I need to feel important or valued."
  - Success Measures – When our relationship is working well, which of each other's and organizational KPIs do we expect to positively impact?
  - Derailers – What would constitute a deal breaker – an unacceptable violation of the implicit social contract? Something that either of us might do that would threaten to jeopardize – or at least deteriorate – an otherwise constructive working relationship?
  - Hygiene Factors – These are additional factors that could inhibit our instincts to collaborate – trust, conflicts or incompatibilities in career direction, working style.
- This kind of analysis can often provide insight as to how to better engage with and satisfy a key stakeholder. As you can see from the form in Appendix vi, it concludes with your identifying an action plan to develop higher levels of engagement and collaboration with each stakeholder.

DESIRED SITUATION

Conducting an effective stakeholder analysis typically provides insight into how you might engage more effectively. It can uncover previously unexpressed yet key needs in a manner that allows you to develop mutual benefit.

(70) TAKE ADVANTAGE OF EXISTING COMPANY NETWORKING FORUMS

Many technical experts hate organizational networking events, thinking their purpose is inauthentic and social. This is nonsense. Internal networking events should be used by Master Experts for corporate and market intelligence gathering. They are a rich source of insight and foresight if approached correctly.

CURRENT & FUTURE ISSUES

Use natural gatherings in your organization to organically and informally meet and build relationships with stakeholders. If you don't do this, you will be faced with the challenge of interfacing with stakeholders only when you want something from them – not a recipe for fostering trust.

SUGGESTED ACTIVITY

- Make a point of actively participating in company networking events – including social occasions such as Friday night drinks. Rather than staying in the comfort zone of hanging out with your friends, make the most of the relaxed setting to seek out new stakeholders to connect with. Develop a short introductory spiel – "Hello, I'm (name). I work in (dept). We're currently working on (brief description of a valued activity). I gather that you work in (stakeholder's team). I'm eager to know more about (something that their team is working on that genuinely interests you)."
- Show an interest in their goals and challenges and, if possible, discover ways that you can add value.
- Take a view that internal networking events are really intelligence gathering exercises. With this is mind, talk to colleagues from departments that you don't usually get a chance to meet. Develop a set of questions so you can understand what challenges they face, who they are competing with externally, etc.

DESIRED SITUATION

It can be very effective to establish some warmth and trust with stakeholders before making requests of them. Another benefit (to you and them) is the value of exchanging marketing and business intelligence.

02

HOW TO BECOME A MASTER EXPERT

EXTERNAL NETWORKER

CAPABILITY: STAKEHOLDER ENGAGEMENT
EXPERT ROLE: EXTERNAL NETWORKER

MASTER EXPERT	• Actively networks beyond the boundaries of the organization to build alliances. • Has a strong grasp of current and emerging needs of key stakeholders external to the organization. • Strategically prioritizes time and attention on the relationships that might add future value.
EXPERT	• Occasionally networks beyond the boundaries of the organization. • Demonstrates limited knowledge of current needs of key stakeholders external to the organization. Little or no visibility of future needs. • Does not spend time on relationships that may have future value.
SPECIALIST	• Network focus is almost completely internal. • Little or not connection to stakeholders external to the organization. • Focuses on immediate, internal relationships.
DERAILING	• External relationships are typically in the professional domain, and focused on technical knowledge and developments. • Future value is defined as personal career value rather than organizational value.

(71)

ACTIVELY PARTICIPATE IN WELL-CHOSEN NETWORKING EVENTS

Our own organizations are bubbles in their own right. Unless we know what is going on in other organizations, we can't possibly assess whether we are adding the value we ought to be. Smart selection of relevant networking events achieves this objective.

CURRENT & FUTURE ISSUES

Networking beyond the boundaries of your own organization, or you will end up with a narrow and institutionalized view of the world. By networking more broadly, you get to understand what is going on in the rest of your profession or industry and can parlay that back into creating value in your organization.

SUGGESTED ACTIVITY

- Decide how much time you are prepared to invest in building your external network. For some, it might be one evening per week. For others, one evening per month or per quarter. Research which networking events or associations are most advantageous for you to participate in. Choose judiciously. Where will you most likely encounter your target stakeholders? How many people typically attend and what calibre are they? Are there presentations of educational merit planned?
- Where the event text ticks enough boxes, enrol and attend. When you attend, don't be shy. Explore people's goals and challenges and consider ways you might add value or collaborate for mutual benefit. Develop a spiel: ""Hello, I'm (name). I work for (organization). We're currently working on (brief description of a valued activity). I found the presentation on (speaker's topic) interesting in the following ways ... What about you?"
- Aim to make at least one interesting connection each time. Take your business cards and ask for theirs. Where there is an emergent area of mutual interest, follow up and see how things work out.

DESIRED SITUATION

External networking can be extremely rewarding in terms of broadening your outlook. It will make you more aware of trends in your industry and adjacent industries, challenges others are facing, and successful alternative strategies.

72

CHANGE YOUR READING HABITS AND EXPLORE NEW VISTAS

Bubbles exist in many forms – and reading habits are one of them. If all we read about is what is happening in our limited technical domain we are destined to operate at a transactional specialist level for our entire career.

CURRENT & FUTURE ISSUES

To broaden your horizons and not be one-dimensional. Many technical experts focus most of their attention in terms of information gathering on staying current in their technical specialism. This tends to make conversations with colleagues from different technical domains difficult – there is usually little common ground to discuss.

SUGGESTED ACTIVITY

- Even if you are a technical specialist, understanding current challenges and emerging trends in different disciplines is often illuminating. For example, how are breakthroughs in science changing the way organizations operate? How is the private exploration of space going to change the way in which previously state funded exercises can be executed.
- Learn at least a little about what trends are happening in other domains. For example, if you intersect with the risk team, google 'new trends in risk' and take 15 minutes to scan the major issues risk managers are facing today and into the future.
- This will help you to understand the risk team's concerns better, and enables you to have an informed conversation with one of the risk team at the next networking event. Usually, the trends in other technical domains resonate with what is going on in your domain as well.

DESIRED SITUATION

Being more widely informed helps you navigate the organization and build better relationships with key stakeholder groups. Understanding the challenges of other domains often produces unforeseen insights into changes and challenges your own domain might face.

73 ATTEND ADJACENT EVENTS

We often are so concerned about building our technical expertise to a level which is unbeatable, we end up attending (and talking to, and learning from) only people in our field of specialisation (domain). This means we develop a narrow point of view.

CURRENT & FUTURE ISSUES

Current issues you are aiming to prevent or address
To broaden our understanding of the environment in which our organization operates, and our view of adjacent domains.

SUGGESTED ACTIVITY

- Find networking events or conferences that promote content you would not normally focus on but is adjacent enough to be useful. As an example, an HR expert might attend a conference designed for chief digital officers. At this conference they won't talk about HR, but they will talk about the challenges of culture change as an organization digitizes processes and uses digital to change the way in which the organization connects with employees and customers.
- This wider context is vital if the HR specialist is going to play a Master Expert role in shaping the digital journey of HR in their organization.
- Look for conferences or other events that focus on emerging trends (for example, customer centricity) that are increasingly applying to your world.
- Build your capability to assess future impact in your domain – how might this trend manifest itself in my industry/specialism? If I was launching a new entity into our space, focused on this trend, how would I try and disrupt my current employer? How might we defend against such an incursion?

DESIRED SITUATION

This strategy both informs us more broadly about challenges that are coming and helps us build a more eclectic network of specialists in other domains.

03

HOW TO BECOME A MASTER EXPERT

NETWORK MANAGER

CAPABILITY: STAKEHOLDER ENGAGEMENT
EXPERT ROLE: NETWORK MANAGER

MASTER EXPERT	• Relationship with key stakeholders is as a strategic partner and trusted technical thought leader. • Relationships always generate mutually beneficial outcomes. • Anticipates future needs. • Manages conflicting priorities and requirements among stakeholders for win-win, holistic organizational wide outcomes.
EXPERT	• Relationship with key stakeholders is as a trusted technical partner, providing timely advice and direction. • Relationship mostly generates mutually beneficial outcomes. • Anticipates current needs. • Manages conflicting priorities and requirements among stakeholders for win-win, department outcomes.
SPECIALIST	• Relationship with key stakeholders is as an on-demand technical supplier. • Reacts to immediate needs. • Is not yet adept at managing conflict priorities and requirements.
DERAILING	• Perceived by key stakeholders as difficult to deal with, and unapproachable. • Service is provided inconsistently and unreliably.

74 BUILD A COMPREHENSIVE STAKEHOLDER MAP

Experts work in highly complex ecosystems that are shifting and adapting all the time. Master Experts work hard to get a handle on their stakeholder groups, and take a strategic approach to prioritization.

CURRENT & FUTURE ISSUES

For us to be able to strategically manage our stakeholder relationships, we need to know who our stakeholders are, and assess and qualify their importance to us, and therefore the amount of time that each requires from us. Without a comprehensive stakeholder map, we can't begin to manage our highly complex expert eco-system.

SUGGESTED ACTIVITY

- Build a stakeholder map, mapping all stakeholder relationships (by individuals not by departments). Consider all the work you do in a typical month and ask who you interact with. Pay particular attention to invisible stakeholders – those on whom you depend to complete your work but may not regularly interact with except on a remote and transactional basis. Some of your most important stakeholders may be junior to you. A typical expert will have at least 60 to 80 individuals on their stakeholder map when it is fully populated. Note that it may take you several days to remember everyone.
- Maintain the currency of your stakeholder map by reviewing it periodically.
- Consider how you are going to manage the relationships you have mapped. It is impossible to give even time to 80 people, so some will need to be prioritised, and others you'll need to develop an informal routine to stay in touch without these interactions taking much time.
- Later growth ideas concern auditing your key relationship.
- Ask yourself who is not on your stakeholder map that you would like to be?

DESIRED SITUATION

You move from a reactive, stressed management of your key stakeholders to a strategic, planned, and effective approach. You know who your stakeholders are, and how often you need to interact with them to maintain excellent, win-win stakeholder relationships. Your stakeholder map is also future focused, containing relationships you intend to build in the future to advance your impact and career.

75 PERIODICALLY SURVEY YOUR STAKEHOLDERS

In the dynamic world in which we now live, things change fast. Such as stakeholder imperatives and priorities and expectations of service. Master Experts are constantly taking the pulse of key stakeholders.

CURRENT & FUTURE ISSUES

Frequently update your understanding of stakeholders' changing needs, preferences and priorities. Otherwise you run the risk of missing emerging requirements and having your services and solutions becoming outdated and obsolete.

SUGGESTED ACTIVITY

- Seek feedback on your services and update yourself on your stakeholders' needs, priorities, plans and challenges. Use the consolidated data to shape you and your team's direction, feedback and services. Feedback can come in the form of ad hoc conversations or surveys.
- Ask structured questions at the beginning or the end of every stakeholder interaction.
- Examples:
  - "What are we going to have to do differently in the future?"
  - "What was working before but isn't now?"
  - "What was important before but is now less important, and what has this priority been replaced by?"
- Seek other existing internal data feeds that the organization may have in order to understand in more detail what is changing in the organization.

DESIRED SITUATION

Continuously refreshing your understanding of your stakeholders' needs and priorities will allow you to remain relevant and establish in their minds that they are important to you.

(76)

BE A CONNECTOR

If you are dependent on others to deliver great work, you'll want to make sure they are as connected as you are, and they should be. Being a connector achieves this objective.

CURRENT & FUTURE ISSUES

Actively help others build their internal networks. They are likely to reciprocate. Your stakeholders don't exist in a vacuum, but are part of a network where there are likely advantages of their being connected with each other. You will also be building their capability to deliver great work in partnership with you, and ensuring they don't have blind spots than negatively impact the work they do in partnership with you.

SUGGESTED ACTIVITY

- Make a point of introducing stakeholders to each other where you perceive there is value in their having a more active engagement with each other. Actively promote tighter collaboration between all of you.
- At networking events explore where others fit in to the organization, who they have strong relationships with, and who they would like to have strong relationships with. See where you can assist with an introduction, and where they can assist you in building a connection that you feel would be valuable.

DESIRED SITUATION

By introducing stakeholders who can derive an advantage from working together more closely, apart from the intrinsic benefits arising from their doing so, you will build increased trust and goodwill between each of them and you.

77 ACTIVELY ORIENT YOUR ROLE, AND YOUR TEAM'S ROLE, AROUND DELIVERING VALUE TO KEY STAKEHOLDERS

You have to understand who your most important stakeholders are, and then focus on work that matters most for the stakeholders that matter most. How do you prioritise? This is how.

CURRENT & FUTURE ISSUES

Focus on your stakeholders. When you're maxed out attending to an overwhelming number of requests, it can be easy to lose focus on what really matters. We can often end up with a default focus based on others' demands rather than having a clear sense of mission or purpose.

SUGGESTED ACTIVITY

- Develop a statement of purpose aimed at addressing the prioritized needs of prioritized stakeholders. Ensure you are delivering on it. Ideally, this is something that you would share or even co-develop with them to get their buy-in. This will help you reflect on your core purpose.
- If working with your team, start by scheduling a brainstorming session – allow an hour or two depending on the size of the team. Ask them to share their ideas of purpose and values. Encourage them to be creative and demonstrate that their input is valued. And be sure to allow enough time to explore options. Remember, there are no bad ideas in brainstorming.
- Use the following questions to trigger ideas and discussions about what should be included in your mission statement:
  - What does our team want to be known for?
  - How do we want to treat each other?
  - What kind of workplace do we want to have?
  - What unique talents and skill does each person bring to the team?
  - What do we want to achieve?
  - What unique contributions can we make?
- Then, narrow down the top three to five ideas generated in the brainstorming session. Which ideas are most crucial and valuable? What would those principles look like in practice? See if you can turn these into a succinct statement of purpose. Take the time to run it by stakeholders to gauge their impressions of it.

DESIRED SITUATION

Signalling your focus to others can help you in prioritizing when demand for your time is high. It can assist with decision-making, and with managing expectations.

78 ADOPT A 'PAY IT FORWARD' APPROACH TO NETWORKING

It's time to change the polarity around networking. Considering it a service to others means you need to think about "paying it forward".

CURRENT & FUTURE ISSUES

Get away from the 'what can you do for me' approach to networking. Whether it is internal or external networking it comes across as inauthentic, vaguely manipulative and distasteful. While we know we should be spending more time networking, this mindset gets in the way of us doing it effectively.

SUGGESTED ACTIVITY

- Change your mindset towards objectives at networking events and adopt the principle of 'paying it forward'. Instead of asking what this person can do for me, ask what you can do for them. It might be a connection they need, or an article that you could forward that they might find interesting, or a problem that with a small amount of personal attention you can help them solve.
- Whatever the case, the concept of paying it forward means that you are building a genuine relationship with someone by adding value to them. If they in turn can see a value they can add to you, they will willingly do so. You are giving, not taking.
- Note that this approach doesn't imply that you must receive anything in return, or indeed expect to. Any reciprocation is an added benefit.

DESIRED SITUATION

Random acts of kindness and consideration are much more powerful than we might imagine. These keep you front of mind across your network and build a positive personal brand. You may be positively surprised at how many of your colleagues – and which ones – find ways to reciprocate.

79 FUTUREPROOF YOUR NETWORK

Given our dynamic workplaces, two or three major stakeholders in your work world in 12 months' time are probably not yet on your stakeholder map. How do we make sure we are future-proofing?

CURRENT & FUTURE ISSUES

Ensure your stakeholder map reflects not just where you currently sit in the organization, but where you are going. We want to be constantly alert for changes in the organisation which mean we need to build new relationships and identify future stakeholders. We want to avoid being blindsided by sudden changes in agenda which negatively impact our domains, without having had the chance to influence.

SUGGESTED ACTIVITY

- Ask yourself who is currently not on your stakeholder map, but you would like to be. Take some time to consider who might be useful or necessary for you to have a good relationship with in the near future, for you to achieve your professional goals. These stakeholders may be internal or external.
- Ask yourself who will make the decision on who gets responsibility for exciting new projects that you would like to be involved with. Are they on your stakeholder map? How well do you know them, and more importantly, how aware are they of your capabilities and aspirations to contribute more? Who might be involved in the next reorganization or restructure, and are they aware of the contributions you currently make and aspire to make?
- Develop a practical plan for building relationships with these new stakeholders that add value to them as well as you. If these stakeholders are more senior than you in the organization, you'll need to find ways interface with them that add value to them. An example might be asking them to assess and validate initiatives you are taking to align your work with strategic direction, or organizational roadmap.

DESIRED SITUATION

A future focus on the people who will be able to assist you fulfil your potential in your organization will help you focus on impact tomorrow as well as impact today.

80 RESET A BROKEN STAKEHOLDER RELATIONSHIP

Everyone has broken stakeholder relationships. The standard mindset is that it was somehow "their fault". Master Experts are focused on repairing sub-optimal relationship as soon as possible, and understanding that part of the reason it is partially or fully broken is us.

CURRENT & FUTURE ISSUES

Repair broken or suboptimal stakeholder relationships and find win-win settings. Most experts have stakeholder relationships that for one reason or another have become negative relationships, where the parties don't collaborate or communicate as they should. This means the value that the two parties could add is not being delivered.

SUGGESTED ACTIVITY

- The easiest part of this growth opportunity is to identify which stakeholder relationships are operating sub-optimally. Once identified, conduct an audit of the relationship. What are your objectives and what are theirs? How will this stakeholder help you achieve your KPIs and how will you help them achieve theirs? What is their working style, what's yours, and how aligned or mismatched are they? What actions taken by your stakeholder annoy you the most, and why?
- Now ask the question in reverse – what do you do (or not do) that annoys your stakeholder? Many experts when faced with these questions make assumptions about what the other party might say if asked. This is a fatal error. You need to know just what they are thinking.
- The first conversation or contact with the estranged stakeholder is the hardest. Be transparent and honest about your reason for wanting to reconnect and reset the relationship. You can use many openings:
  - "I'd like to get updated on your priorities these days, and my part in helping you achieve your professional goals."
  - "I feel that between us we could add more value if we understood each other and our goals better. Would you be open to an informal conversation about this?"
  - "There have been changes in my priorities and I'd like to update you and get an update on yours as well."
- Note that all these questions are future-focused, not focused on solving past problems.
- Ask yourself what you might need to change to improve the relationship. Both parties must change their attitudes and ways of working to achieve a better relationship. It is not just you asking them to change.

DESIRED SITUATION

Broken stakeholder relationships consume extra energy that most of us don't have time for. Resetting means less stress and pressure, and a happier and more productive relationship. This means both parties can add more value to each other and the organization.

There is usually a redemptive feel to a reset relationship. It feels good and creates positive energy. Once you have reset one relationship you'll be keen to do so again with the next less performing stakeholder relationship.

COLLABORATION

Acts as a valuable, proactive member of their team, virtual or co-located, taking on a leadership role when required and appropriate.

THE THREE EXPERT ROLES OF COLLABORATION

TEAM WORKER

A culturally effective team player, from local and technical to global and organizational.

COMMUNICATOR

Displaying advanced communication skills from rational influence and technical descriptions, to sophisticated influencing skills, with both technical and business fluency.

DIPLOMAT

Enabling fast and informed decision making, managing negotiations, all from a facilitative leadership approach, supporting win-win prioritization and outcomes.

01
TEAM
WORKER

02
COMMUNICATOR

03
DIPLOMAT

01

HOW TO BECOME A MASTER EXPERT

TEAM
WORKER

CAPABILITY: COLLABORATION
EXPERT ROLE: TEAM WORKER

MASTER EXPERT

- Acts as a valuable member of many teams; encouraging collaboration and a focus on team outcomes.
- Works across organizational boundaries in a highly effective manner.
- Has a keen understanding and interest in individual and team member goals and motivations.
- Masterful at working globally in virtual, multi nation, and multi cultural teams.

EXPERT

- Acts as a senior individual contributor on one or two teams, playing the role of expert advisor rather than active team player.
- Works collaboratively with many stakeholders.
- Understands the motivations of all team members, and works to align with own motivations.
- Progressing to work effectively with multiple nationalities and cultures, embracing diversity.

SPECIALIST

- Acts as an individual contributor on a team.
- Works mostly alone, on allocated tasks.
- Understands and responds to own motivations.
- Comfortable working with familiar nationalities and cultures.

DERAILING

- Prefers to work alone, and may appear disconnected and distant from teams.
- Works autonomously, with a focus on personal agenda. Competitive rather than collaborative; wishes to be seen as the most expert.
- May be culturally insensitive or uncaring.
- Demonstrates higher levels of engagement with technical profession than the organization.

81 ADOPT ONE OR MORE INTENTIONAL VALUE-ADDED ROLES IN THE TEAMS YOU PARTICIPATE IN

Master Experts don't just offer advice when asked, they lean in and help out teams in other (non-required) ways. This builds team effectiveness and the experts' personal brand.

CURRENT & FUTURE ISSUES

Take up a deliberate and expanded role within your teams. Otherwise you relegate your participation to providing detached advice. This will make you appear one-dimensional and aloof, or even unwilling to shoulder or share responsibility. Your teams miss out on the additional value that you could add.

SUGGESTED ACTIVITY

- Experts often find themselves participating in many teams. The precise expectation of their contribution to the team is often undefined but the implicit expectation (on the part of the experts and also the others in attendance) is that they are purely there to represent their field of expertise. This can result in a passive level of participation – where the role of driving the meetings' optimal outcomes is left to others.
- There are a number of additional value-adds that an expert may be able to help a team with in order that it functions optimally such as:
  - Helping to steer meetings efficiently and effectively.
  - Championing relationships.
  - Coaching and facilitating.
- Experiment with participating in one or more of the teams you engage with via one of the deliberate and significant roles described more fully in Appendix viii. These may remain informal roles that you play.

DESIRED SITUATION

Adopting an expanded role will not only help optimise team performance and morale, but also foster increased trust and collaboration between you and team members.

82 GET TO KNOW PEOPLE BETTER

If your relationship are purely transactional then you'll never build the required trust in stakeholders to build a truly win-win engagement. Some experts think brief conversations about things such as 'how was your weekend" is a waste of time. Master Experts know they are wrong.

CURRENT & FUTURE ISSUES

Move beyond the pressures of meeting everyday deliverables to work on a more informal and personal connection with your stakeholders. This builds mutual warmth and trust, which are critical foundations for effective collaboration.

SUGGESTED ACTIVITY

- Ask the people in your team about their personal and professional goals. Build a connection beyond the necessities of getting stuff done. Such conversations can easily be informally started over a coffee.
- Build a system to capture the knowledge you have gathered. This makes it easy to remember for the next time you have a meeting – check in on their family, goals etc. This interest needs to be genuine, not simply a career tactic, if it is to be successful in building trust and warmth.

DESIRED SITUATION

Developing mutual warmth and trust lays the foundations for effective collaboration. You may even find you have some interests in common.

83

CLARIFY YOUR TEAM'S PURPOSE

Team purpose isn't just clarified when teams come together for the first time. Things change, and checking back in on purpose is a critical component of maintaining energy, direction, and engagement.

CURRENT & FUTURE ISSUES

Refocus and redefine if necessary your team's sense of purpose. Though teams are typically initially constituted with a defined purpose and outputs, once they have been in place for some time, it's not uncommon for their original reason for existence to get lost amidst business as usual demands. This can make the teams a little dysfunctional. They lose focus, which usually means they lose effectiveness.

SUGGESTED ACTIVITY

- Initiate a conversation within each of your teams about how they contribute to the organization's aims. How clear is their line of sight? Does the team have a scorecard which clearly illustrates its contribution? Does the team's work clearly align to organizational strategy? How does it contribute?
- Consider whether you must participate in zombie projects. They're not quite dead, but they nearly are. Ask the same question about headless projects. The sponsors have long since departed, but the project hasn't done a review of whether it should continue.
- One of the hardest decisions is whether a project should be continued. But asking the hard questions can be courageous and help define and strengthen your personal brand. In reviews conducted by our clients, they typically tell us that at least a quarter of these projects fail the 'should continue' test.

DESIRED SITUATION

Teams that routinely revisit and refresh their sense of purpose tend to have increased vitality and productivity. They also avoid mission drift.

02

HOW TO BECOME A MASTER EXPERT

COMMUNICATOR

CAPABILITY: COLLABORATION
EXPERT ROLE: COMMUNICATOR

MASTER EXPERT

- Brings to life complex technical concepts/terms via compelling story telling in accessible language.
- Inspires and consults, promoting an inclusive processes whereby everyone is heard.
- In-demand presenter across the organization due to ability to combine technical and business concepts.
- Advanced listening skills.

EXPERT

- Translates technical concepts/terms into practical and accessible language to increase others' comprehension.
- Employs a variety of influencing techniques to gain commitment to ideas and plans.
- Takes the lead in delivering effective presentations on behalf of function.
- Good listening skills.

SPECIALIST

- Communicates predominately using technical language.
- Uses rational and policy arguments when influencing technical groups; rarely consults with the wider organisation.
- Rarely takes the lead in technical presentations.

DERAILING

- Communicates almost exclusively using technical language/jargon.
- Favours rational persuasion as primary influencing strategy.
- Comes across as close-minded and opinionated, either by talking far more than listening, or by being non-communicative.

84 IMPROVE AND PRACTISE YOUR PUBLIC SPEAKING – BOTH PLANNED AND IMPROMPTU

Every expert wants to be able to influence more effectively. Unfortunately, proficient public speaking – whether to scary committees or larger groups – is a necessary skill for Master Experts. A skill that takes work and practice.

CURRENT & FUTURE ISSUES

You need the confidence and ability to present your ideas fluently, cohesively, intelligibly and impactfully. Otherwise you will have difficulty influencing effectively.

SUGGESTED ACTIVITY

- Consider joining and participating in your local Toastmasters group or similar to build your confidence, experience and proficiency in communicating, particularly in front of groups of people.
- Use every reasonable opportunity to pitch your ideas within the organization. Make sure you prepare beforehand. Ask colleagues to provide honest and robust feedback, so you can see the positive and negative impacts of your technique and style, and improve them if possible.
- Develop an ability to think deeply about the audience you are about to present to, and what they are really interested in. You do not have to go into great detail when you present to them. Their time is as scarce as yours. Make every minute count by considering what they will find valuable and what level of detail they really need. We often see experts pitching to senior executive teams and missing what the audience really wants. They add unnecessary detail, they don't get to the point quickly enough, they don't connect with the organizational strategy.
- A good starting point is to consider what your audience needs to achieve to get their bonus or promotion or to achieve other aims. Make sure that what you are saying or selling has a direct connection to those outcomes.

DESIRED SITUATION

As your effectiveness in conveying ideas increases, so will your influence. You will be sought out for your ideas and participation in direction-setting conversations.

An improvement in your presentation skills – that is, if you learn quickly and act on feedback – will have an immediate and positive impact on personal brand.

85 DEVELOP AN ELEVATOR PITCH

What do you do? Why do you do it? How does it contribute? Why should I care? Weak experts will struggle to answer these questions "off the cuff". Master Experts will smoothly answer in a compelling manner, and use the opportunity to quickly influence the questioner. Not because they are naturally charismatic, but because they've done the work.

CURRENT & FUTURE ISSUES

Have a short and easy to understand explanation of what you do and why it matters. If you are unable to do this succinctly, the value and nature of what you do will remain a mystery to people.

SUGGESTED ACTIVITY

- Imagine you find yourself in the elevator with a key stakeholder. You have only 30-60 seconds to convey to them, in a relevant and inspiring way, what you do, how it adds value, and why it's important. What would you say?
- Take the time to develop your short statement. Use a story or metaphor if possible. Practise delivering it regularly with different stakeholder groups. Appendix ix provides a structure that you might find helpful.

DESIRED SITUATION

Becoming effective at delivering an elevator pitch will allow you to quickly engage stakeholders. You will be able to convince them of the merits of what you do and the value of collaborating with you.

86 DEVELOP THE ART OF UNSTRUCTURED CONVERSATION

Experts love structure – that's why we are experts. Unstructured conversations fill many of us with terror. How can you plan for an unstructured conversation that occurs without warning? It turns out we can!

CURRENT & FUTURE ISSUES

Become better at general conversation. Experts are often so technically-focused and methodology-driven that it can be less natural to engage in a more relaxed, emergent and free-flowing conversation. This can be intimidating to others – or at least serve to discourage more informal and organic exchanges with stakeholders.

SUGGESTED ACTIVITY

- Invite colleagues or other stakeholders to join you for a coffee. Enquire about their passions and interests and actively listen to them.
- Develop a set of open questions that you can pull from your memory bank and work in almost any environment. Some of our favourite examples are:
  - "What's been changing in your professional world?"
  - "What have been the biggest challenges in the last couple of weeks?"
  - "What are some of your recent successes?"
  - "What are your biggest priorities these days?"
- And, after a presentation at a conference: "What did you think of that presentation?"

DESIRED SITUATION

Effectively developing the art of unstructured conversations will allow you to rapidly build warmth and trust with stakeholders – paving the way for greater collaboration.

87

PRACTISE APPLYING EMPATHY

Communication is a two way process, and it is not just about understanding what someone has just said to you, it is about understanding why they just said it. Do we understand what they are thinking and feeling, as well as what they are saying? We need to practice the art of empathy to fully understand colleagues, in order to serve them better.

CURRENT & FUTURE ISSUES

Listen and empathize. Experts who don't listen effectively are seen as indifferent or even arrogant, not understanding and not caring. They can often end up jumping to solutions before getting the whole story, and leaving their stakeholders feeling they have not been listened to.

SUGGESTED ACTIVITY

- Whenever you encounter stakeholders who are expressing heightened emotions or frustration, use it as an opportunity to be empathetic. Try paraphrasing their concerns before making a counterpoint or trying to solve their problem.
- Focus on understanding how colleagues and stakeholders are feeling as much as what they are saying. If you're not sure what emotions are going on, ask them. "How does this make you feel about how we are tracking on this project?" "Do you have a good feeling about this recommendation, and if not, what is worrying you about it?" "How are we feeling about this decision – do we all feel comfortable that we've made the right decision and we'll be successful, or do we feel slightly differently?" Experts are used to dealing in the black and white of facts and data – but humans are successful or not because of the way they feel about things. Make sure you are getting both sets of data.

DESIRED SITUATION

Listening empathetically builds trust and encourages greater disclosure. As you develop increased expertise in listening with empathy, you are likely to get more buy-in to your proposals, foster increased collaboration, develop a fuller understanding of stakeholders' issues and needs and thus develop more effective solutions

88 BECOME A STUDENT OF GREAT COMMUNICATORS

If you are referencing this guide then you already know that simple rational persuasion alone, doesn't win arguments or get recommendations approved. The "way" in which we communicate is a critical success factor.

CURRENT & FUTURE ISSUES

We want to avoid not having our arguments and recommendations properly heard because we have deficient communication skills. We want to be able to impact value creation more by being able to win over people by the way in which we deliver our viewpoint or business case.

SUGGESTED ACTIVITY

- You come into contact at work with many people who are effective communicators. This isn't a DNA thing – your colleagues have learned how to communicate effectively. You must do the same – become students of the people who communicate well. You should use your expert smarts to figure out what techniques great communicators are using to win arguments. How do they couch things so that they get people's attention?
- You should become a student of Aristotle, and his pyramid of influence – using a combination of personal credibility, emotional connection, and facts (in that order), and make sure you are thinking about how you communicate using this model.
- You should read some of the many great books available on improving business communication. We would highly recommend Say it like Obama, and Putting Stories to Work, and How to Deliver a TED talk.
- You should watch some of the most watched TED talks and consider what techniques these presenters use to communicate effectively (hint: they tell compelling stories).

DESIRED SITUATION

An increased ability to communicate clearly and effectively, getting your point across, and connecting appropriately with your audience. Increased confidence in talking to larger groups.
Understanding that great communication is about preparation, understanding the audience, and technique – and that anyone can learn to do it effectively.

03

HOW TO BECOME A MASTER EXPERT

DIPLOMAT

CAPABILITY: COLLABORATION
EXPERT ROLE: DIPLOMAT

MASTER EXPERT	• Diplomatically negotiates and facilitates win-win outcomes when faced with competing priorities or deadlines. • Focuses on organizational outcomes. • Expert at leading without authority, assisting teams to make good decisions that accelerate results and foster great teamwork.
EXPERT	• Uses formal decision making techniques to arrive at good decisions about priorities and solutions that balance the needs of stakeholders. • Tends to focus on technical outcomes. • Takes on a leadership role when required, comfortable leading with or without authority.
SPECIALIST	• Is involved in making decisions, but rarely takes a leadership role. • Sees issues from a narrow and technical perspective.
DERAILING	• Adopts a combative style when negotiating for outcomes. • Takes an entirely technical view of issues and priorities. • Seeks to get outcomes that are personally favourable, rather than considering broader organizational needs.

(89) SET UP INFORMAL SERVICE LEVEL AGREEMENTS (SLAs)

What makes the world a very stressful place for almost everyone is a lack of agreement about expectations and the ability to maintain service levels. Agreements clarify and reduce conflict.

CURRENT & FUTURE ISSUES

Clarify your stakeholders' expectations. If you and your stakeholders don't know what to expect from each other it's easy for trust to become strained as one or both parties' needs aren't adequately addressed. The purpose is to avoid unnecessary conflict caused by poor communication.

SUGGESTED ACTIVITY

- Develop a mutually-beneficial Service Level Agreement (SLA) with key stakeholders to ensure that your needs and theirs are better understood, communicated and met. Explain that you'd like to ensure that expectations and needs are clearly understood both ways for mutual benefit. It doesn't need to be a formal document – an exchange of emails may be sufficient.
- The Win/Win Agreement Framework might be helpful:

DESIRED RESULTS	• What deliverables does each party commit to? • What are the standards or measures of success? • What outcomes are both parties committed to?
GUIDELINES	• What parameters do both parties agree to abide by? • What protocols exist if there is any variance from the target deliverables? • How much variance is acceptable?
RESOURCES	• What resources does each party need reasonable access to in order to successfully discharge its responsibilities?
ACCOUNTABILITY	• How often, when and how should progress (or performance to target) be reviewed?
CONSEQUENCES	• What happens in the event of success? Overachievement? Underachievement? • What corrective measures are appropriate if required? When and how do they kick in?

- Don't have these conversations in a combative fashion. Your goal is to develop a mutually rewarding relationship, not set up walls or the basis for future recriminations. Clarifying expectations, and delivering accordingly, is a great basis for excellent stakeholder relationships.

DESIRED SITUATION

When stakeholders contract with each other – and agree on mutual expectations – they lay the foundations for greater mutual fulfilment of priorities and needs.

90 DON'T TAKE CONFLICT PERSONALLY

If you are pushing hard for change and innovation, conflict is inevitable. It only becomes disruptive conflict if the parties don't handle it well – for example, taking the push-back on ideas or plans personally. Master Experts turn conflicts into opportunities to learn and to build relationships, not destroy them.

CURRENT & FUTURE ISSUES

Proactively manage conflict. Conflicts arise naturally. If you lack the capability to proactively deal with them then they tend to fester, wearing away at your goodwill with stakeholders and disrupting collaboration.

SUGGESTED ACTIVITY

- If you are experiencing tension with another team or key individual, then undertake a quick needs or situation analysis. Ask yourself a few questions to work out why it has occurred:
- What kind of conflict is this?
- Is it a real clash or just a misalignment of interests?
- Is it because of someone's unmet needs?
- Is it a clash of ideologies and beliefs, or of different styles, standards or values?
- Suspend personal feelings such as frustration, anger, feeling under attack and so on. Conflicts in an organizational environment occur all the time, and we are judged not by the conflicts we are involved in but how we manage those conflicts and seek to find resolution. This doesn't mean giving in – or staying resolutely in our own position – it involves working out the conflict and seeing if a win/win resolution is available.
- Be prepared to have an adult, but calm, conversation with those with whom you are in conflict. Acknowledge that you are, and jointly explore two things – what we agree on, and what we don't agree on. Use the I-GRROW model to understand both parties' realities, which if you are in conflict, will be different.
- Use any emerging insights to work together for mutual success.

DESIRED SITUATION

Addressing conflicts swiftly and masterfully smooths the way for high levels of collaboration. "It also allows you to build relationships because if conflict is managed well, it builds trust. "

91 INVEST IN EMOTIONAL BANK ACCOUNTS

What behaviour from you towards your stakeholders destroys trust? Which behaviours build it? Can you do less of the former and more of the latter?

CURRENT & FUTURE ISSUES

Actively take the initiative to foster high trust relationships. Otherwise the general trend is one of entropy – a gradual deterioration in the natural levels of trust. In extreme cases, when one or both parties' needs are not being addressed – there can even be resentment or antipathy, which undermines collaboration.

SUGGESTED ACTIVITY

• Target specific stakeholder relationships that you feel need improving. Assess the historic balances of deposits and withdrawals into the Emotional Bank Account. Identify some deposits (trust building activities) that you can make and withdrawals (trust eroding activities) you can reduce, eliminate or at least offset.

COMMON EXAMPLES OF DEPOSITS INTO THE EMOTIONAL BANK ACCOUNT	COMMON EXAMPLES OF WITHDRAWALS FROM THE EMOTIONAL BANK ACCOUNT
Taking the time to listen to people, attending to – or at least showing sensitivity towards – their needs.	Interrupting, not listening, judging, being callous towards their needs, sparing them no time.
Making and keeping commitments, accepting responsibility, taking ownership and initiative.	Resisting making commitments, breaking commitments, excuses, blaming, an unwillingness to accept responsibility or ownership.
Eliciting, clarifying and honouring expectations.	Making assumptions, violating expectations.
Common courtesies, thoughtfulness, sincere apologies.	Rudeness, indifference, oversight.
Being trustworthy, honourable, reliable, loyal to the absent, honest, authentic, candid, courageous.	Being untrustworthy, dishonest, unreliable, gossipy, fake, cowardly.

91 INVEST IN EMOTIONAL BANK ACCOUNTS CONTINUNED

SUGGESTED ACTIVITY

- It's likely that, if a particular relationship isn't working well at present, you will have some grievances with the other party's historic conduct. The Emotional Bank Account framework invites you to take the initiative to improve the relationship.
- That doesn't mean that you entirely overlook your own needs. But it means that you take the initiative to start making deposits into your emotional bank account with the other party even if they don't seem initially deserving or responsive.

DESIRED SITUATION

By consciously investing in key relationships – by building trust one interaction at a time – you will develop increasing mutual trust with stakeholders, laying the foundations for improved collaboration.

PERSONAL IMPACT

Influences others positively, is self aware, empathetic and adaptive, and makes individual and collective results happen

THE THREE EXPERT ROLES OF PERSONAL IMPACT

POSITIVE INFLUENCER

Making positive contributions, avoiding cynical and disengaged behavior, instead being inspiring and warm, and demonstrating a can-do attitude.

SELF AWARE ADAPTER

Aware of their position within the organizational context, very aware of their personal impact on others, and caring.

RESULTS DRIVER

Demonstrating a results orientation, combining advanced prioritization and on-time delivery of agreed outcomes and value

01
POSITIVE INFLUENCER

02
SELF AWARE ADAPTER

03
RESULTS DRIVER

01

HOW TO BECOME A MASTER EXPERT

POSITIVE INFLUENCER

CAPABILITY: PERSONAL IMPACT
EXPERT ROLE: POSITIVE INFLUENCER

MASTER EXPERT

- Exudes personal warmth, empathy and patience when dealing with colleagues from outside their technical domain.
- Presents as positive and 'can do' even when challenging thinking and solutions.
- Inspirational—exudes passion for the vison and mission.

EXPERT

- Appears supportive and patient towards those who lack technical depth.
- Articulates arguments in a measured way, presenting as constructive even when saying no.
- Motivational—articulates the vision and mission of the organization effectively.

SPECIALIST

- Empathetic towards technical cohort, but struggles to be empathetic to broader stakeholder group.
- Articulates arguments in a rational manner, which can appear negative when saying no.
- Self motivational—struggles to connect work to the vision and mission.

DERAILING

- Can present as condescending and egotistical when dealing with colleagues from outside their technical domain.
- Presents as disengaged and cynical.
- Demotivational— does not connect work to vision and mission of the organization.

92 INCREASE YOUR RANGE OF INFLUENCING STRATEGIES

Every expert has default influencing strategies that they turn to nearly all the time. But we have many different strategies we could choose from – and should. Failing to influence and then continuing to use the same influencing strategies is, well, insanity.

CURRENT & FUTURE ISSUES

Consider the many different motivations people have. Often experts rely on a limited range of influencing strategies. Being rationally inclined, they lean towards rational persuasion – purely facts, sound reasoning, tight logic, etc. This may not always prove effective – logic and reasoning are not the only factors driving people's decision-making.

SUGGESTED ACTIVITY

- Identify one or more situations (or people) where you'd like increased influence. Define the outcomes that would result from this increased influence. Identify which methods of influence (see Appendix x) you have historically sought to employ in this situation that haven't proven sufficiently impactful. Identify which alternative tactics you could experiment with next time.
- Although each of the nine influencing methodologies has their potential merits in different situations, a few of them are more likely to be effective: inspirational appeal, consultation and personal appeal. Some strategies are more likely to result in resistance – pressure, coalition (peer pressure) and rational persuasion.
- Personal appeal is only a useful option if you have significant equity in the relationship to begin with. In cashing in some of that equity you might be making a small withdrawal from the emotional bank account.
- Consulting can be very effective, provided there's a genuine openness towards whatever emerges from the consultation. People tend to feel that their needs, opinions and ideas have been duly considered and thus be emotionally warmer to whatever conclusion emerges.
- Inspirational appeal requires insight and courage, or at least self-confidence.
- You have to get a reasonable sense of what the person you're seeking to influence values and show how what you're proposing will effectively address those interests.

DESIRED SITUATION

Selecting from a wider range of influencing strategies increases the likelihood of getting buy-in. You will develop the expertise to know which to select in different situations and how to effectively deploy them.

(93) SEEK TO ENGAGE PEOPLE BY LINKING YOUR PROPOSALS TO THEIR NEEDS

Colleagues we work with engage more with projects and people that motivate them. We need to consider what the felt needs of our colleagues are and pitch our proposals to them with their motivations in mind.

CURRENT & FUTURE ISSUES

Position your proposals to positively impact the needs of your stakeholders, or they will be regarded as irrelevant or low value. In the competition for finite time and resources, poorly positioned proposals will lose out to those that more obviously address felt needs.

SUGGESTED ACTIVITY

- When you're seeking to engage others and get their buy-in to a project or initiative, show how it will heighten the likelihood of their own needs being addressed. This will require significant analysis and careful thought. How well do you understand their most keenly felt needs?
- Felt needs often go beyond mere functional requirements. They can include such things as:
  - The need to feel safe and secure.
  - The need for comfort, balance or convenience.
  - Perceived value for money.
  - The need for a certain quality of life.
  - The need to feel adequately resourced and equipped.
  - The need to feel supported, cared for and belonging.
  - The need to feel a sense of achievement, progress, recognition, importance, being heard, being trusted, feeling autonomous.
  - To feel stimulated, a sense of variety.
  - The need for a sense of meaning and purpose.
  - It tends to be unmet needs that are most strongly felt. Satisfied needs prompt no feelings of insufficiency and tend not to be 'felt needs'. Often people will provide clues as to what their strongest felt needs are in their language and behavior patterns.
  - How well does the course of action that you've laid out in your proposal meaningfully address such felt needs in the people you're seeking to engage? Sometimes, poorly thought through initiatives not only fail to address felt needs but can even violate them. Can links be credibly made?

DESIRED SITUATION

When people perceive a strong connection between what you're proposing and their felt needs, they are less likely to resist. They are more likely to buy-in and commit (the necessary time, commitment, resources, etc).

94 # DEVELOP A HABIT OF FOCUSING ON YOUR CIRCLE OF INFLUENCE

Stressing about matters which you have very limited (or no) ability to control is a waste of energy. Master Experts focus on matters where they can make a difference, and usually do.

CURRENT & FUTURE ISSUES

Consider how you can best influence those around you. Experts can often feel disempowered because they lack formal authority. Rather than exploring what influence they might have on a situation, they get overwhelmed by all the factors that lie beyond their control.
Their apparent lack of direct authority to compel others, make decisions, allocate resources can result in a general lack of 'agency'.

SUGGESTED ACTIVITY

• Rather than being overwhelmed and paralyzed by how complex and challenging circumstances are, focus positively by asking what are all the possible moves you could make. Pick the most effective option from amongst whatever list of options this enquiry generates.

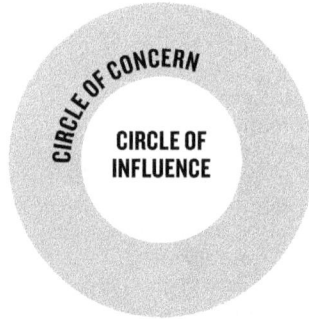

CIRCLE OF CONCERN

CIRCLE OF INFLUENCE

• Distinguish between a focus on things that concern us but which we can't do much about (things in our Circle of Concern) and those things that we can do something about (things in our Circle of Influence). Positive influencers – as the term suggests – are resourceful and don't get overwhelmed or discouraged by adverse circumstances. They focus their time and energies on taking actions that lie in their Circle of Influence.

DESIRED SITUATION

People who focus on their Circle of Influence tend to be more productive, because they're always positively focused on what they can do rather than feeling disempowered by all the things that they can't influence. They tend to gradually enhance their influence – and others respond positively to them.

02

HOW TO BECOME A MASTER EXPERT

SELF AWARE ADAPTER

CAPABILITY: PERSONAL IMPACT
EXPERT ROLE: SELF AWARE ADAPTER

MASTER EXPERT	• Excellent at managing own and others emotions. • Aware and caring about personal impact on others. • Able and willing to adapt communication style to engage effectively with others. • Shows humility.
EXPERT	• Manages own emotions effectively. • Aware and caring about personal impact on others. • Some ability to adapt communication style to others. • Shows humility.
SPECIALIST	• Developing ability to manage own emotions. • Learning to be aware of personal impact on others. • Focused on own communication style. • May present as self-important while establishing expert credentials.
DERAILING	• Poor at managing own emotions. • Does not care about or is unaware of personal impact on others. • Quickly shoots down ideas they don't agree with in a negative manner.

95 INCREASE YOUR SELF-AWARENESS TO REDUCE INEFFECTIVE BEHAVIOR

Do you really know how you are experienced as a colleague? Have you really thought about the impact your actions (and inaction) has on colleagues and stakeholders? Have you taken the time to consider increasing your awareness of how you impact the work and workplace of those around you?

CURRENT & FUTURE ISSUES

Become more aware of the effect you have on others. When experts lack self-awareness, they can often exhibit behaviors that undermine their relationships with stakeholders.

SUGGESTED ACTIVITY

- Seek feedback from others – when are you being effective in your interactions with others, and when are you being ineffective? The courage to seek honest feedback enables you to significantly impact your effectiveness.
- Consider undertaking an Expertship360 survey – a feedback tool designed by experts for experts that provides outstanding actionable data.
- Identify situations where your behavior is less emotionally intelligent than is ideal. A helpful self-assessment can be found in Appendix Vi. Try to pinpoint the specific triggers that prompt your suboptimal behavior.
- Reflect on and plan what alternative responses you'll choose in future. When those envisioned triggers occur, pursue your planned alternative responses rather than reacting based on your feelings in the moment.

DESIRED SITUATION

People with high self-awareness are able to adjust their attitudes and behavior so as to engage with others effectively. They engage constructively – immunized against the sway of negative feelings in themselves or others. This builds trust and influence.

96 UNDERSTAND WHAT MOTIVATES THOSE AROUND YOU (AND YOURSELF)

To what extent are you really clear about what motivates you? For many experts, they are clear on what de-motivates them, but the precise things which generate incremental additional effort are more elusive. A study of what drives you forward helps you motivate yourself, and provides clues into what drives others.

CURRENT & FUTURE ISSUES

We want to avoid making the mistake of believing that the motivations of the people we are surrounded by are the same as everyone else's motivations. Statistically, this is very unlikely.

SUGGESTED ACTIVITY

- Read up on the standard human motivators and consider carefully what motivates you. Is it job security? Is it financial reward? Is it achievement of great work? Is it the ability to work with autonomy? Are your motivations a combination of some of these?
- Start observing colleagues and considering what motivates them. If not sure, then in conversations with them explore what is going on in their lives, as this often provides a clue as to their underlying motivation.
- Start to take into account what motivates colleagues when working with them and when seeking to influence them or build trust. Emphasising that we'll all get a bonus when this work is completed won't work for someone who is motivated by autonomy, for example.
- Consider what motivates key stakeholders and consider how that might affect the way in which you should approach them and the way in which you work together.

DESIRED SITUATION

The more you understand what drives the colleagues and customers you work with, the better you will be able to build effective working relationships with them. If you understand what they value, this allows you to focus on adding real value rather than guessing what they might find valuable (often a default position seen among experts).

97 UNDERTAKE AN EMOTIONAL INTELLIGENCE SELF-ASSESSMENT

The successful Master Expert operates with a potent cocktail of high IQ combined with well-developed EQ – emotional intelligence. Well developed because EQ can be developed. How hard are you working on your EQ? And do you understand the benefits of doing so?

CURRENT & FUTURE ISSUES

Work on your emotional intelligence. People with suboptimal emotional intelligence tend to lack both the personal discipline to be individually effective as well as the people-smarts to engage with and influence others. The expression of problematic emotions is a major derailer.

SUGGESTED ACTIVITY

- Read and undertake the assessment in Emotional Intelligence 2.0 (by Bradbury/Greaves) and identify any areas that can be improved upon. This book contains some great recommendations as to how each of the Emotional Intelligence dimensions can be developed.
- Once you have the results of your assessment, commit to work on two or three areas where you believe there will be a bit pay off by improving your emotional intelligence. You may need to elicit the support of close friends or work colleagues to help you shape (and get feedback) on these initiatives.
- Study the data on emotional intelligence and how, as professionals progress into more and more senior positions in organizations, emotional intelligence becomes more important than IQ. Understand the impacts of being effective or ineffective in this capability.

DESIRED SITUATION

Increasing your emotional intelligence will improve your individual effectiveness, as well as your ability to engage with and influence others. You'll also understand people and outcomes better, and this decreases stress and offers up opportunity to approach things (and people) differently.

98 COMMIT TO LIFE-LONG LEARNING

In today's world things change all the time. That means we need to too. Experts operating on last year's insights are this year being outsourced. If you really want to be a Master Expert, you need to commit to life-long learning.

CURRENT & FUTURE ISSUES

In order to stay at the top of your game, you need to invest in yourself. We are seeking to avoid getting left behind by changes in our fields and our organizations and the way they operate. We seek to be seen as still contemporary in both knowledge and approach.

SUGGESTED ACTIVITY

- This Guide is all about having a plan, executing it, knowing what you are trying to change, the reasons why, and what the impact will be. Our templates for Personal Growth Plans help you do this but underneath all the templates and growth suggestions needs to be a genuine desire and commitment to understanding that lifelong learning isn't just a nice to have, it is essential for continued relevance in today's dynamically changing world. If you are reading this Guide simply because either your boss or Human Resources told you, you won't succeed in making any worthwhile changes. You've got to believe it matters.
- As an expert, you have probably committed a great deal of time to mastering technical skills. The vast majority of personal growth ideas explained in this guide focus on enterprise skills – the additional skills that when layered over your technical skills help you deploy those technical skills more effectively. Your lifelong learning should be two thirds enterprise skills, one third technical skills in order for you to attain the status of Master Expert.
- We strongly encourage you to explore learning in adjacent areas – that is, outside your current work discipline.

DESIRED SITUATION

Prioritising time in your schedule for learning – particularly around enterprise skills – will pay many dividends. You'll feel you are progressing, you'll be adding more value, and if you spend some time studying adjacent disciplines, you'll discover new approaches to your work that maintain quality and renewal.

03

HOW TO BECOME A MASTER EXPERT

RESULTS
DRIVER

CAPABILITY: PERSONAL IMPACT
EXPERT ROLE: RESULTS DRIVER

MASTER EXPERT	• Drives relentlessly for results and delivers real world outcomes. • Considers interests of wider organization and customers. • Takes ownership for technical and associated business outcomes. • Manages time effectively to focus on important and urgent matters, but favouring the important. • Deploys courage in having transformative conversations with colleagues.
EXPERT	• Frequently engages beyond minimum requirements. • Considers interests of self, and others, and of the organization. • Takes responsibility for allocated technical outcomes. • Manages time effectively to focus on important and urgent matters in equal measure.
SPECIALIST	• Delivers acceptable results or productivity in line with expectations. • Considers interest of self and others. • Takes responsibility for allocated tasks. • Learning to manage their own time effectively.
DERAILING	• Constantly makes excuses for lack of delivery. • Considers interests of self above all other interests, focused on own agenda. • Generally blames other colleagues or departments for unachieved outcomes. • Prefers to work alone, and can fail to maintain effective contact with rest of the team.

99

TAKE OWNERSHIP FOR IMPROVING KEY ORGANIZATIONAL RESULTS

Many experts do the work that is required and then wash their hands of the big picture outcome, as if they have no responsibility for the larger outcome. Master Experts want to know what the large outcome is, and takes ownership for making sure all the work is done, not just their bit.

CURRENT & FUTURE ISSUES

Focus on the results the organization needs, beyond your immediate perspective. If you don't seem aware of or committed to improving organizational results, you will be seen as a marginal player.

SUGGESTED ACTIVITY

- Identify which organizational KPIs you have the ability to influence. Align your contributions to positively impact them. Track and report any uplifts in those metrics that you can reasonably attribute to your inputs.
- Constantly clarify success measures for the projects you are working on. Ensure that the stakeholders, sponsors and yourselves are completely aligned about what success looks like, and what would be considered failure.
- Deploy SMART goal setting techniques to ensure that everyone – but most importantly yourself – understands what needs to be delivered by when and by whom (Specific, Measurable, Agreed, Realistic, and Time-Bound goals). Be very clear on which KPIs you own or contribute to. A model to help you set SMART goals can be seen in Appendix Xi.
- Avoid the blame game – it is everyone else's fault that something hasn't been delivered on time, on budget or to agreed specification. You're a player in this game, take responsibility for making things happen.

DESIRED SITUATION

By positively impacting organizational results, you will be viewed as a vital business contributor and not just a mere technical boffin.

(100) BECOME A MASTER PRIORITIZER

The great challenge of experts is having many masters and many projects running simultaneously, with many conflicting priorities and deadlines. The ability to be exceptional at prioritizing, and to have everyone understand why, is a marvellous skill to master.

CURRENT & FUTURE ISSUES

We want to avoid being constantly overworked, missing deadlines, feeling pressure to get a body of work done that is impossible to do in the time we have. We want to avoid the negative behaviors and mindsets that come from believing more senior people do not appreciate our predicament. We'd like to spend time on the tasks that matter most – and deliver most value. We'd like to be able to make a strong case that is respected and acted upon to our multiple masters to achieve this.

SUGGESTED ACTIVITY

- Learn how to say no diplomatically and credibly. Our masters will continue to give us tasks until we say no. Until we say no they will believe, erroneously, that we have time to deliver on these tasks because we haven't had the courage – or technique – to explain that we can't. But just saying we're busy won't usually get the result we want – more realistic deadlines, or the work being allocated elsewhere, or additional resources being deployed to assist us.
- Use your calendar for tasks as well as meetings. This means that your calendar becomes a clear single page view of what you are working on. If you simply put meetings in, then colleagues will fill up your diary with other meetings. If you need two hours to develop a project plan, that goes into your diary. This enables you to manage new requests more effectively – you can show how busy you are, and negotiate different timelines or responsibilities.
- Deploy negative gearing – what won't get done and why? Assuming your workload takes up 110 per of your time this week already, a new request can't feasibly get done, unless something else doesn't get done. Invite your stakeholders to choose which tasks they wish to delay, in order for you to prioritize their new task. Develop techniques that enable all of your masters to see the whole of your workload and make sensible decisions about priorities with you.
- Get all of your masters on the same page in terms of your workload. If one master doesn't see the workload from another master, it will be impossible for them to appreciate the conflicting priorities.

DESIRED SITUATION

Developing a system of capturing all the work you do and being able to make a case for refusing extra work leads to better work life balance, greater engagement, and a feeling of fairness. It is important for your health and wealth. Playing victim and accepting all work presented to you without pushing back diplomatically conversely is the road to disengagement and despair.

101 TAKE INITIATIVE WHERE COURAGEOUS CONVERSATIONS ARE NECESSARY

Experts destined for a life of disgruntlement and disappointment avoid having the courageous conversations they need to have with colleagues and stakeholders. Master Experts step up to the plate and have diplomatic but real conversations – and everyone benefits from their courage.

CURRENT & FUTURE ISSUES

Tackle challenging conversations in a timely and effective way. Otherwise issues will remain unaddressed and your needs will not be met. This can lead to resentment and looking weak and ineffectual. We are seeking to avoid avoidance.

SUGGESTED ACTIVITY

- Rather than refraining from expressing your concerns or needs, which tends to result in resentment, find a way to express your needs, concerns, observations in a manner that balances courage and consideration.
- Focus on listening carefully to the other point of view. After all, it's a conversation that you're after. A framework that will help you do this is included in Appendix Vii.
- Focus on impacts and outcomes not activities. What is the impact of this deadline being missed, or the quality of work being substandard? What impacts are there down the line, elsewhere in the organization, that we can't see but if we could, we'd realise are material – important and requiring of us to do better?
- Choose a conversation you have been avoiding, and using the I-GRROW framework, plan the conversation carefully, and then make it happen.

DESIRED SITUATION

Mastering the art of courageous conversations will enable you to have increased influence and impact – including the timely resolution of issues.

(102) MAKE A HABIT OF PRACTISING THE SIX STEP WEEKLY PLANNING PROCESS

Holding yourself accountable for what you want to achieve in any one day or week is an important part of making sure you are doing the right work, for the right people, for the right reasons. Anything else is just being reactive to whoever shouts loudest and longest.

CURRENT & FUTURE ISSUES

Develop a planning discipline that prioritises high-value strategic activities over the merely urgent. This will prevent you from getting caught up in day-to-day demands at the expense of long-term effectiveness.

SUGGESTED ACTIVITY

- Ensure that you set and deliver meaningful, proactive, well-defined, high-impact important-but-non-urgent goals each week. A step-by-step process for doing this is illustrated and explained in detail in Appendix Xiii.
- Develop a disciplined routine to set targets and check whether they have been achieved.
- Manage stakeholder expectations by sharing your priorities.
- Help multiple stakeholders understand that they all make competing demands of you, and this process is how you prioritise which works comes first and why.

DESIRED SITUATION

The regular practice of the Six Step Planning process will allow you to gradually transform the content of your appointments diary and To-do list to be of increasing strategic value – not merely 'busyness'.

APPENDIX
I-XII

APPENDIX I
PERSONAL GROWTH PLAN

GROWTH OPPORTUNITY	
DATE:	**VERSION:**
CURRENT SITUATION	
BEHAVIORS	**IMPACTS**
DESIRED SITUATION	
BEHAVIORS	**IMPACTS/PAYOFFS**

	ACTIVITY	TIMEFRAME	MEASURE OF SUCCESS
1			
2			
3			
ACCOUNTABILITY STRATEGY			
1			
2			

APPENDIX II
A MODEL FOR INNOVATION

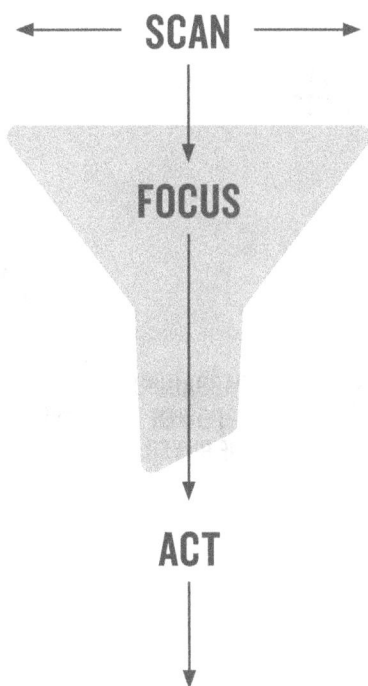

SCAN

FOCUS

ACT

Scanning involves:
- Looking at historic and predictive data that highlight problems to be solved or opportunities to be capitalised upon.
- Finding out what important stakeholders think is valuable or problematic and how your products/services measure up.
- Seeing if you can anticipate future needs and challenges – asking "What next?"
- Thinking through all kinds of possible actions and the potential upside or downside implications for your business – asking "what if".
- Generally being inquisitive and curious.

Focusing involves:
- Selecting, from amongst all the potential problems and opportunities identified in the SCAN, which ones are most valuable – and feasible – to solve/address.
- Gathering the relevant evidence on precisely what needs improving – and establishing/agreeing improvement criteria.
- Finding out why the problem exists, what's been done to fix it previously and how or why that did or didn't work out.

Acting involves:
- Working out precisely how to solve the problem or capitalise upon the opportunity – developing a hypothesis to be tested.
- Testing out one's hypothesis and monitoring and reporting outcomes.
- Developing a proof of concept and s elling it for wider adoption.

APPENDIX III
PORTERS FIVE FORCES ANALYSIS

NEW ENTRANTS

RIVALRY DETERMINANTS:
- Industry growth
- Fixed (or storage) costs/value added
- Intermittent overcapacity
- Product differences
- Brand identity
- Switching costs
- Concentration and balance
- Informational complexity
- Diversity of competitors
- Corporate stakes
- Exit barriers

BARRIERS TO ENTRY:
- Economies of Scale
- Proprietary product differences
- Brand identity
- Switching costs
- Capital requirements
- Access to distribution
- Absolute cost advantages
  - Proprietary learning curve
  - Access to necessary inputs
  - Proprietary low-cost product design
- Government policy
- Expected retaliation

THREAT OF ENTRANTS

INDUSTRY COMPETITORS
INTENSITY OF RIVALRY

SUPPLIERS

BUYERS

BARGAINING POWER OF SUPPLIERS

BARGAINING POWER OF BUYERS

THREAT OF SUBSTITUTES

DETERMINANTS OF SUPPLIER POWER:
- Differentiation of inputs
- Switching costs of suppliers and firms in the industry
- Presence of substitute inputs
- Supplier concentration
- Importance of volume to supplier
- Cost relative to total purchases in the industry
- Impact of inputs on cost or differentiation
- Threat of forward integration relative to threat of backward integration by firms in the industry

SUBSTITUTES

DETERMINANTS OF SUBSTITUTION THREAT:
- Relative price performance of substitutes
- Switching costs
- Buyer propensity to substitute

DETERMINANTS OF BUYER POWER:

BARGAINING LEVERAGE:
- Buyer concentration versus firm concentration
- Buyer volume
- Buyer switching costs relative to firm switching costs
- Buyer information
- Ability to backward integrate
- Substitute products
- Pull-through

PRICE SENSITIVITY:
- Price/total purchases
- Product differences
- Brand identity impact on quality/performance
- Buyer profits
- Decision makers' incentives

APPENDIX IV
CHANGE CURVE

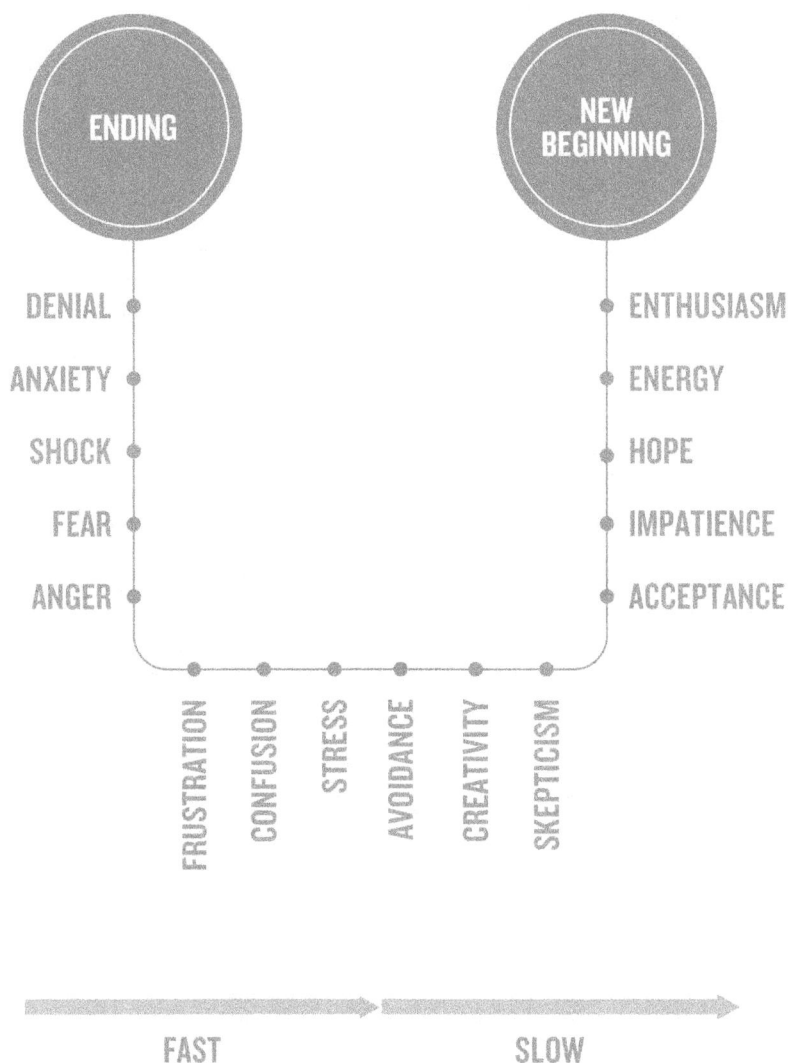

ENDING

NEW BEGINNING

DENIAL

ANXIETY

SHOCK

FEAR

ANGER

ENTHUSIASM

ENERGY

HOPE

IMPATIENCE

ACCEPTANCE

FRUSTRATION

CONFUSION

STRESS

AVOIDANCE

CREATIVITY

SKEPTICISM

FAST

SLOW

APPENDIX V
KOTTER'S 8 STEP CHANGE MODEL

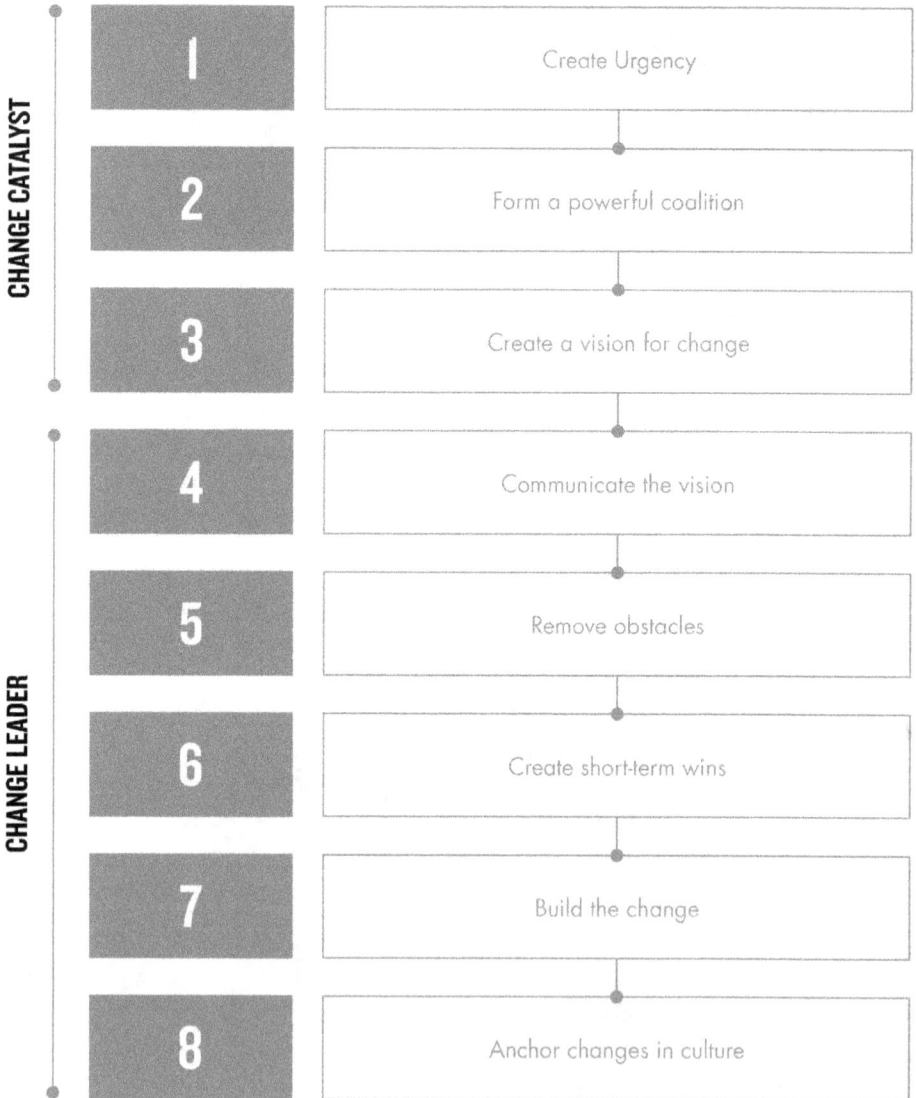

CHANGE CATALYST

1	Create Urgency
2	Form a powerful coalition
3	Create a vision for change

CHANGE LEADER

4	Communicate the vision
5	Remove obstacles
6	Create short-term wins
7	Build the change
8	Anchor changes in culture

SPECIFIC WAYS THAT YOU CAN CONSTRUCTIVELY CONTRIBUTE TO CHANGE INITIATIVES

There are several ways that experts can participate in change initiatives:

- Initiating/Leading Change – often as a consequence of innovation or continuous improvement, an expert might seek to change mindsets, processes, practices, structures, methodologies, etc. The 8 steps below are especially important for someone leading/initiating change as one cannot necessarily depend upon anyone else taking up or leading change management activities.
- Being a Change Catalyst – though the expert may not have initiated the change – or primarily accountable for its successful implementation – he/she nonetheless chooses to proactively take up responsibilities in assuring a smooth transition from the current to the desired state (beyond being a good corporate citizen and participating). Kotter's 8 steps also provide practical guidance as to the kinds of contributions that can be useful
- Being a Change Participant – at the very least, a proactive expert will not resist change but be a constructive supporter. Kotter's 8 steps should also provide helpful reference. John Kotter is a renowned thought leader on the topic of change having written several bestselling books on the topic. Here are 8 best practice steps that all help contribute to a successful transition from the "current state" to the "target state".

1. Create Urgency

Since most people resist change – moving from the known to the unknown – there needs to be a compelling case as to why the change is necessary (e.g. the problematic consequences of staying as we are or the compelling upside of changing). Those initiating the change need to win over hearts and minds. The perceived benefits of changing need to outweigh any perceived disadvantages. Without creating a compelling case, there will be no momentum to overcome any resistance. Even if an expert didn't happen to initiate the change, he/she can always help build/strengthen the case and thus elicit others' buy-in. This can include such activities as:

- Identifying potential **threats**, and **develop scenarios** showing what could happen in the future.
- Examining **opportunities** that should be, or could be, exploited.
- Starting honest discussions and give dynamic and convincing reasons to get people talking and thinking.
- Requesting support from customers, outside stakeholders and industry people to strengthen your argument.

2. Form a Powerful Coalition

The momentum building can be accelerated if the change initiative is seen to have the initial support from key opinion leaders. Identifying early adopters and others with influence who can become positive advocates for and ambassadors of change will sway others. This can include such activities as:

- Identifying the true leaders in your organization, as well as your key **stakeholders.**
- Asking for an emotional commitment from these key people.
- Working on team building within your change coalition.
- Checking your team for weak areas and ensure that you have a good mix of people from different departments and different levels within your company.

3. Create a Vision for Change

While much is made of the need for a "burning platform" – i.e., the supposition that people won't move unless the ground beneath them is on fire – it is equally, if not more, important to clearly define the destination to be arrived at. People need to know what success looks like – and feel that it will be worthwhile (offsetting any inconvenience involved in the change itself and transition period). What you can do:

- Determine the **values** that are central to the change.

- Develop a short summary (one or two sentences) that captures what you "see" as the future of your organization.
- <u>Create a strategy</u> to execute that vision.
- Ensure that your change coalition can describe the vision in five minutes or less.
- Practice your "vision speech" often.

4. Communicate the Vision

People often must hear a message several times before a) it connects and b) they recognise that you're intent to change is serious. What you can do:
- Talk often about your change vision.
- Address peoples' concerns and anxieties, openly and honestly.
- Apply your vision to all aspects of operations – from training to performance reviews. Tie everything back to the vision.
- Lead by example.

5. Remove Obstacles

If implementation feels too hard then people's commitment to see the change through may waver. The nay-sayers may feel empowered to mount increased resistance if they run into stumbling blocks. What you can do:
- Identify, or hire, change leaders whose main roles are to deliver the change.
- Look at your organizational structure, job descriptions, and performance and compensation systems to ensure they're in line with your vision.
- Recognize and reward people for making change happen.
- Identify people who are resisting the change and help them see what's needed.
- Take action to quickly remove barriers (human or otherwise).

6. Create Short-Terms Wins

People's sustained commitment – especially over longer durations – will be aided if they experience the benefits early and often. It's all about reducing the need for leaps of faith and the risks of scepticism. What you can do:
- Look for sure-fire projects that you can implement without help from any strong critics of the change.
- Don't choose early targets that are expensive. You want to be able to justify the investment in each project.
- Thoroughly analyse the potential pros and cons of your targets. If you don't succeed with an early goal, it can hurt your entire change initiative.
- Reward the people who help you meet the targets.

7. Build the Change

Don't celebrate success too early. The change needs to be truly bedded in. What you can do:
- After every win, analyze what went right, and what needs improving.
- Set goals to continue building on the momentum you've achieved.
- Learn about kaizen , the idea of continuous improvement.
- Keep ideas fresh by bringing in new change agents and leaders for your change coalition.

8. Anchor the Changes in Corporate Culture

It's not over until the change is embedded into new everyday habits and behaviors. What you can do:
- Talk about progress every chance you get. Tell success stories about the change process and repeat other stories that you hear.
- Include the change ideals and values when hiring and training new staff.
- Publicly recognize key members of your original change coalition, and make sure the rest of the staff – new and old – remembers their contributions.
- Create plans to replace key leaders of change as they move on. This will help ensure that their legacy is not lost or forgotten.

APPENDIX VI
STAKEHOLDER ENGAGEMENT HEALTH CHECK

RELATIONSHIP:	IMPORTANCE:

PURPOSE	What is it? Level of clarity?
1	From my perspective	
2	From my stakeholders' perspective	

SUCCESS MEASURES	What are they? SMART goals?
3	From my perspective	
4	From my stakeholders' perspective	
5	From the organizations' perspective	

DE-RAILERS	What are they? Impact?
6	From my perspective	
7	From my stakeholders' perspective	

HYGIENE FACTORS	What are they? Impact?
8	Do we trust each other?	
9	Do our aspirations enhance or inhibit us?	
10	Do our individual styles align or clash?	

OVERALL SCORE	1 = Extremely poor, 10 = superb
11	Do we trust each other?	1 2 3 4 5 6 7 8 9 10
12	Action Plan	

APPENDIX VIII
THE FIVE TEAM ROLES OF EXPERTS

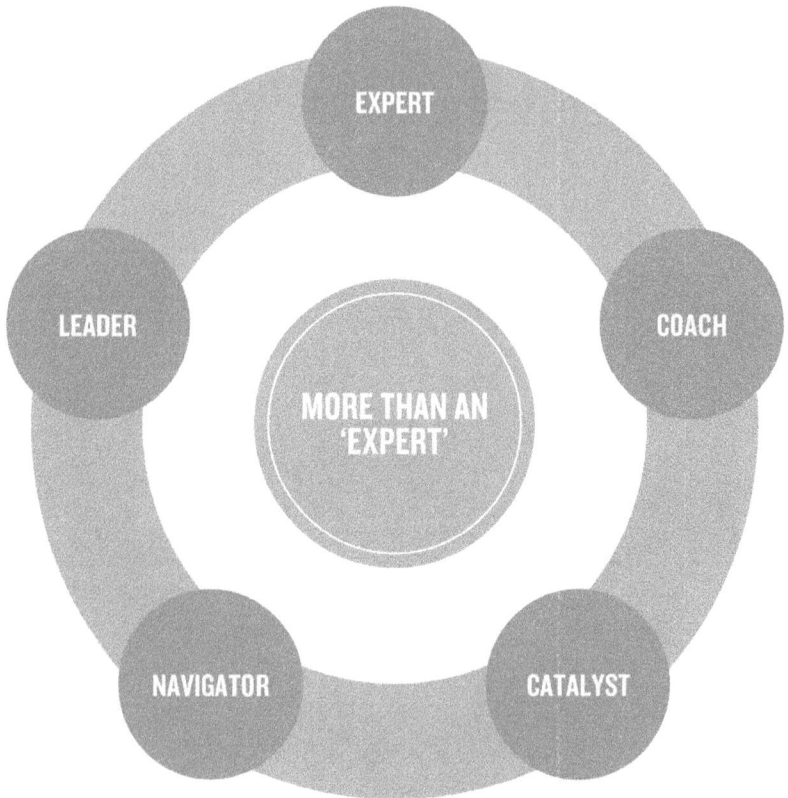

1. The Role of an Expert

- This is the role that is usually the basis of the expert's inclusion in a given team. Given the expert's depth of professional/technical knowledge in a given field, their perspective (and therefore inclusion in a team) is often considered essential when related matters are being discussed.
- There is a significant risk that such a role inclines the expert to be more of a "naysayer" (or judge/critic) than "enabler". This corresponds to Meredith Belbin's "Evaluator" where the tendency is less about generating ideas so much as evaluating the relative merits of ideas which others have put forward.
- This role can be also very limiting, where the expert only contributes when their expertise is required, rather than voluntarily expanding their sense of role and contribution to include some of the other roles described on this page.
- There are several additional roles, listed below, that an expert can play rather than this limited, default persona of "technical advisor".

2. The Role of a Catalyst

- A critical role for a Master Expert is that of Change Catalyst– acting as the initiator of change, and setting the change agenda.
- This persona is often assumed to be associated with large scale change projects, with experts contributing at the genesis of major transformations, and this may well be a role Master Experts will play.
- But experts can be change catalysts on an ongoing basis on the teams they operate within. This can take the form of challenging the status quo, challenging enterprise and market assumptions, or challenging the way we have always done things.
- In some instances, experts will be called upon to invent a new way of tackling a complex challenge. Experts can often play a useful role at such times with their designing of a suitable methodology or approach for progressing the task at hand.
- This is an expression of the expert's choosing to help drive business outcomes rather than remaining somewhat aloof as a detached technical advisor.

3. The Role of Navigator

- A critical role for a Master Expert is that of Team Worker – playing an active and valuable role in many teams: promotion and encouraging collaboration and focusing on accelerated team outcomes. There are often times when a team gets stuck, and the nominal leader of the group (perhaps a project manager) needs assistance in moving forward with a deliverable. Often teams get stuck in the details and struggle to progress from exploring conceptual ideas to implementing decisive actions and realising benefits.
- An outcome-minded expert can take responsibility for helping the team to move forward – navigating a way, facilitating the shaping of the team's direction and timeline, the development of clear criteria and a process for timely decision-making, instilling a sense of urgency and a bias for action.
- A further critical role for a Master Expert is that of a diplomat– negotiating and facilitating win-win outcomes when teams are faced with competing priorities or deadlines. This requires the ability to

influence without authority, fostering great teamwork very often between teams. Often the expert is in a unique position to be able to play this role.

4. The Role of Coach

- A critical role for a Master Expert is that of Knowledge Coach – which involves deploying a question-based, collaborative coaching style. Coaching is often considered a standalone activity, but, team meetings and team work provides ample opportunities to coach in the moment.
- Experts have an opportunity to contribute to the team culture as well as the skill sets and mindsets of other team members. This is another way of exercising responsibility rather than seeming hands off, nonaccountable for team-performance or growth of team members.
- Master Experts use every interaction available to share knowledge and explain the "why" behind approaches to build greater understanding. Master Experts can model the key behaviors of high performing team members, demonstrating the ability to listen closely to other team members, facilitate respectful brainstorming sessions, and illustrate the power of great questions to penetrate difficult problems.

5. The Role of Leader

- Two critical roles for a Master Expert is that of Change Leader and Results Driver – the ability to effectively lead change initiatives and drive relentlessly for results, delivering real world outcomes.
- Experts are often in the position of being the most experienced person on a team, without being the formal leader. In order to elevate to the role of Master Expert, the expert has to take on informal leadership responsibilities in a diplomatic way.
- There will be times when the team's need is for increased leadership – even in cases when a team has a formallydesignated person "in charge". Working in tandem with any "powers that be", an expert can assist/drive the team's developing a clear focus and goals, help it progress through project phases, look out for the welfare and development of team members, etc.

APPENDIX IV
ELEVATOR PITCH -
PERSONAL NETWORKING ESSENTIALS

The 1-Minute Introduction

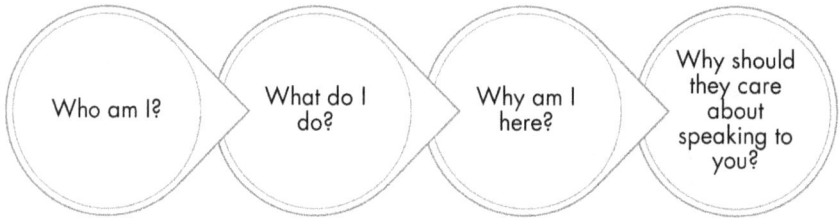

| Who am I? | What do I do? | Why am I here? | Why should they care about speaking to you? |

The 1-Minute Interrogation

| Who are you? | What do you do? | Why are you here? | What have you found interesting? | What are your biggest challenges at work? |

CAN YOU PAY IT FORWARD?

Reverse Networking - 'Paying it forward'

Instead of approaching networking as "what value can I get from them", reverse networking requires a "how might I assist them" philosophy. This immediately positions you are a valuable member of their network, not a drain on their time.

Reverse networking questions:
- Who do I know who might be able to help them?
- What do I know that might be able to help them?
- How did someone help me, and how might I do the same for people in my network?
- What are their biggest challenges and how might I help?

APPENDIX X
INFLUENCING STRATEGIES

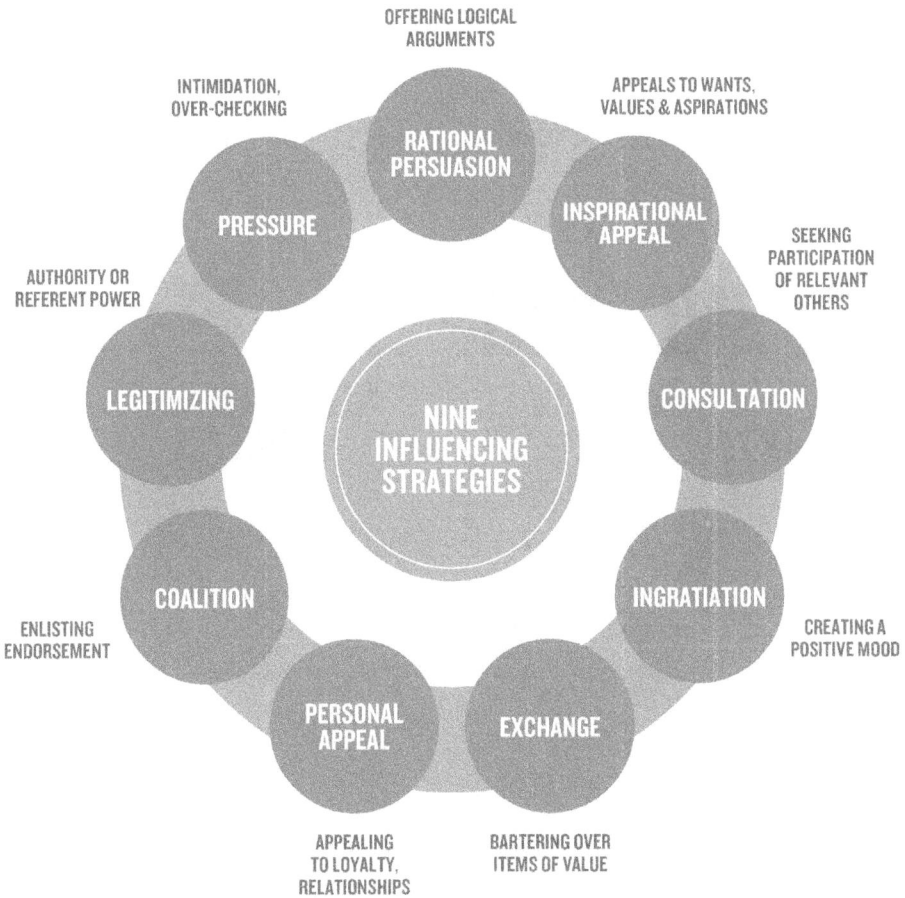

OFFERING LOGICAL ARGUMENTS

INTIMIDATION, OVER-CHECKING

APPEALS TO WANTS, VALUES & ASPIRATIONS

RATIONAL PERSUASION

PRESSURE

INSPIRATIONAL APPEAL

AUTHORITY OR REFERENT POWER

SEEKING PARTICIPATION OF RELEVANT OTHERS

LEGITIMIZING

NINE INFLUENCING STRATEGIES

CONSULTATION

COALITION

INGRATIATION

ENLISTING ENDORSEMENT

CREATING A POSITIVE MOOD

PERSONAL APPEAL

EXCHANGE

APPEALING TO LOYALTY, RELATIONSHIPS

BARTERING OVER ITEMS OF VALUE

Ref: Falbe, C.M. & Yukl, G. (1992), Consequences for Managers of Using Single Influence Tactics and Combinations of Tactics, Academy of Management Journal, 35, 638-652.

APPENDIX XI
THE GENOS MODEL OF EMOTIONAL INTELLIGENCE: SELF-ASSESSMENT

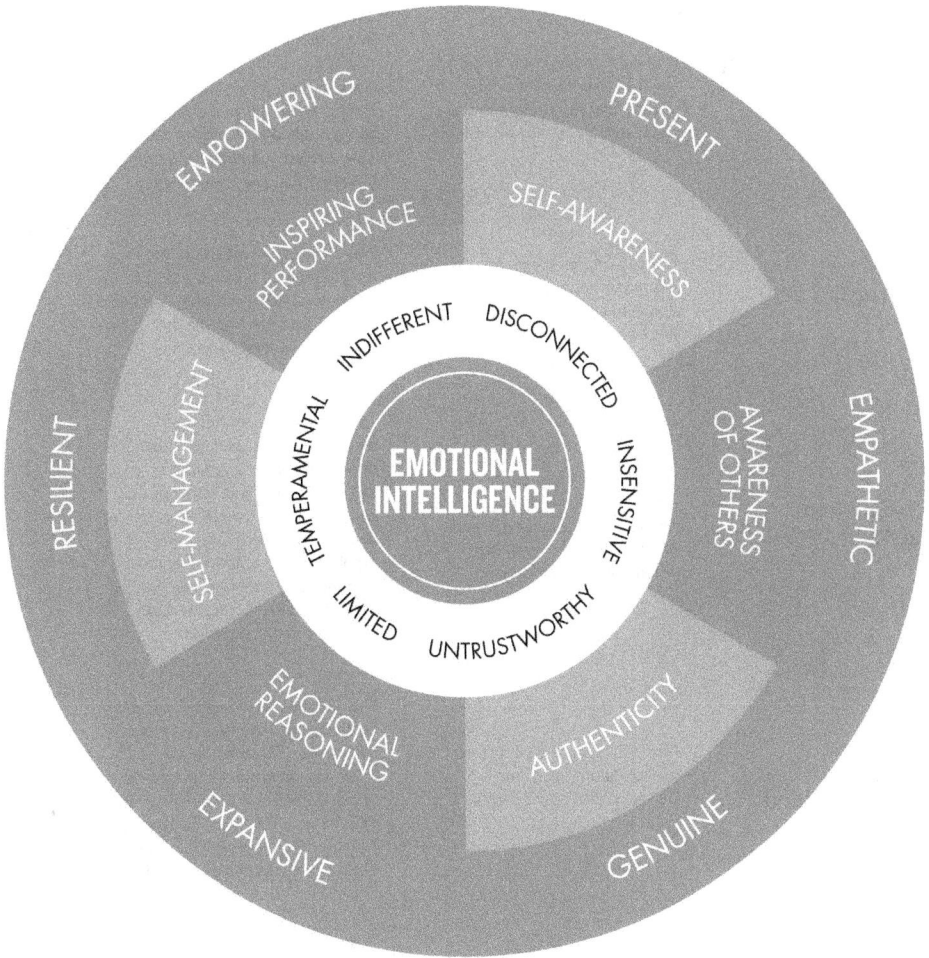

	DEFINITION	HIGH
SELF-AWARENESS	Being aware of the behavior you demonstrate, your strengths and limitations, and the impact you have on others.	When leaders are emotionally self-aware they are present with the role their feelings are playing in their decisions, behavior and performance.
AWARENESS OF OTHERS	Noticing and acknowledging others, ensuring others feel valued and adjusting one's own style to best fit with others.	These leaders identify the things that make people feel productive emotions that drive high performance (emotions such as feeling valued, listened to, cared for, consulted and understood). They are empathetic and create meaning and purpose for others.
AUTHENTICITY	Openly and effectively expressing oneself, honouring commitments and encouraging this behavior in others.	This skill helps leaders create an environment of understanding, openness and trust. Others perceive leaders who are high on this skill as genuine and trustworthy.
EMOTIONAL REASONING	Using the information in feelings (from oneself and others) and combining it with other facts and information when decision making.	These leaders consider their own and other's feelings when making decisions, combining this information with facts, and communicating this decision-making process to others. Combining emotional and rational pieces of information enables leaders to make expansive, creative and well thought-out decisions.
SELF-MANAGEMENT	Managing one's own mood and emotions, time and behavior and continuously improving oneself.	This skill helps leaders be resilient and manage high work demands and stress. These leaders are optimistic and look to find the opportunities and possibilities that exist even in the face of adversity. They generate a positive mood both within themselves and others.
INSPIRING PERFORMANCE	Facilitating high performance in others through problem solving, promoting, recognising and supporting others' work.	This skill equips leaders with the capacity to get colleagues to cooperate and work effectively together. Leaders who can positively influence other's moods, feelings and emotions are empowering to work with and easily motivate those around them.

"Table derived from the Genos Model of Emotional Intelligence, © Genos Pty Ltd"

LOW	SELF-EVALUATION	HOW I MIGHT FURTHER DEVELOP THIS
When leaders are not aware of the influence of their emotions on their decisions, behavior and performance, they are often disconnected.		
Leaders who demonstrate this skill infrequently can come across as being insensitive to the way others feel.		
Leaders who are guarded, avoid conflict, or are inappropriately blunt about the way they feel, can come across as untrustworthy. This can create cultures of mistrust, artificial harmony and misunderstandings.		
When leaders do not use emotional information and focus on facts or technical information only, they tend to be limited in their decision making and could be risking low 'buy-in' of their decisions by others		
When leaders do not engage in emotional self-management they appear temperamental.		
These leaders do not know how to create a positive working environment for others. They don't help people find effective ways of responding to upsetting events or help people resolve issues that are affecting their performance. They appear indifferent to others.		

APPENDIX XII
SMART DEVELOPMENT GOALS

Feedback offers a sense of measure, along with frequency measures and organizational metrics.

Harder and higher goals demand more effort. Challenge is motivating with reward and over-reaching can lead to hesitation if effort not supported.

The goals must be relevant to the individual, team, site and business

One key result with indication of desired performance level.

Timeframes further clarify expectations and support maintenance of momentum.

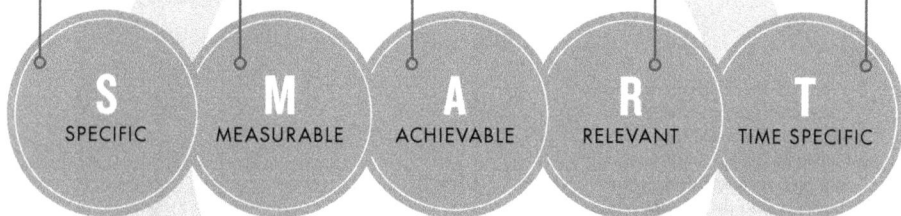

S SPECIFIC

M MEASURABLE

A ACHIEVABLE

R RELEVANT

T TIME SPECIFIC

MOTIVATING

WHAT YOU'RE TRYING TO ACHIEVE IS:
• Clear • Easy to interpret

SUCCESS ON THE OBJECTIVE IS:
• Tangible • Visible • Objective

PERFORMANCE LEVELS ARE:
• Challenging • Attainable

KPI IS:
• Relevant to individual /team /site/business

THE ACTIONS ARE:
• Defined within a clear timeframe

DEMOTIVATING

WHAT YOU'RE TRYING TO ACHIEVE IS:
• Unclear • Confusing

SUCCESS ON THE OBJECTIVE IS:
• Unknown • Subjective

PERFORMANCE LEVELS ARE:
• Too easy • Too difficult

KPI IS:
• Outside employee ability to control

THE ACTIONS ARE:
• Open ended

APPENDIX XII
COURAGE/CONSIDERATION MODEL

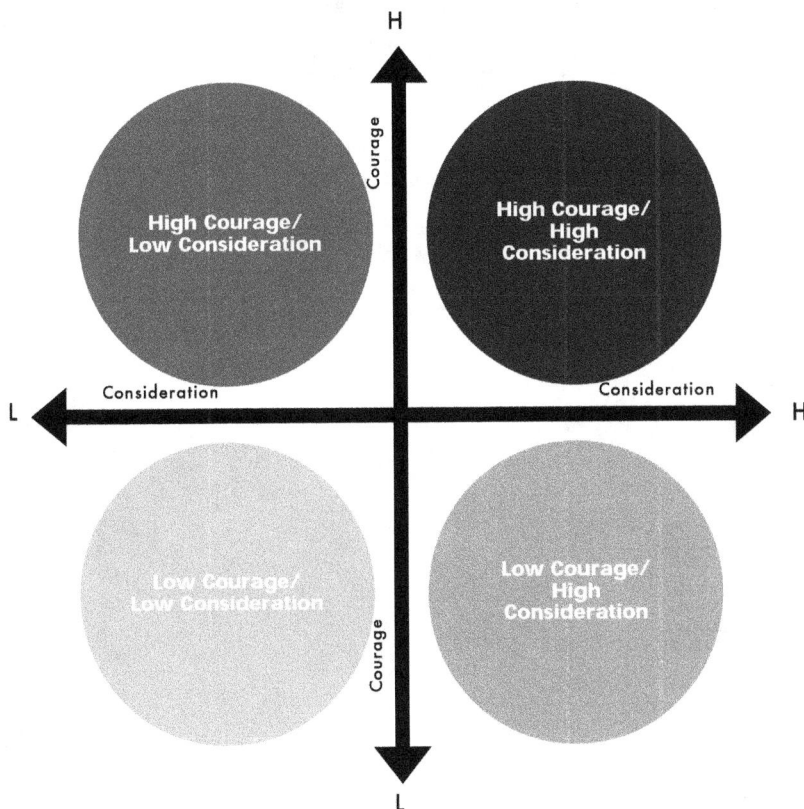

Delivering Highly Courageous and Highly Considerate Feedback

It takes both high levels of skill and character to deliver feedback in such a way as to provoke positive change in another person. Typically, we doubt that there's an effective way to communicate our concerns without provoking defensiveness or retaliation on the other person's part – and we worry that our attempts to provoke their changing will merely result in non-constructive conflict. Such thinking often leads to our withholding what we really want to say – or perhaps "pulling our punches", being indirect, hinting subtly, etc.

Occasionally, having suppressed our frustration and potentially built up some tension and resentment, we can explode and express our frustration so forcefully that our communication becomes counter-productive. The other party reacts to our forceful tone and all prospects of applying emotional intelligence is compromised.

APPENDIX XIII
STEPHEN COVEY'S SIX STEP
WEEKLY PLANNING PRACTICE

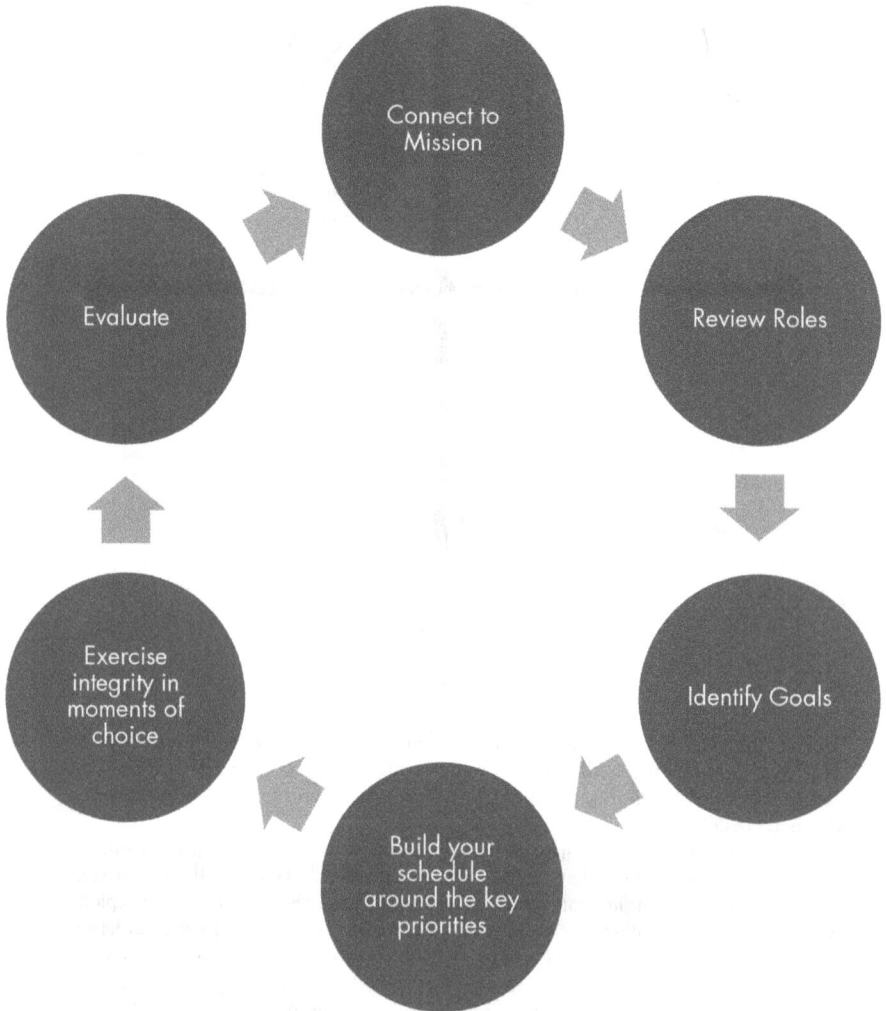

Connect to Mission

Review Roles

Identify Goals

Build your schedule around the key priorities

Exercise integrity in moments of choice

Evaluate

ROLES/GOALS – SIX STEP PLANNING PROCESS

ROLE	GOAL

www.ingramcontent.com/pod-product-compliance
Lightning Source LLC
Chambersburg PA
CBHW061150220326
41599CB00025B/4426